T0300256

ROUTLEDGE LIBRARY EDITIONS: LANDMARKS IN THE HISTORY OF ECONOMIC THOUGHT

Volume 8

PROTECTIVE & PREFERENTIAL IMPORT DUTIES

PROTECTIVE & PREFERENTIAL IMPORT DUTIES

A. C. PIGOU

Routledge
Taylor & Francis Group

LONDON AND NEW YORK

First published in 1906 by Macmillan & Co., Limited

This edition first published in 2017
by Routledge
2 Park Square, Milton Park, Abingdon, Oxon OX14 4RN

and by Routledge
711 Third Avenue, New York, NY 10017

Routledge is an imprint of the Taylor & Francis Group, an informa business

British Library Cataloguing in Publication Data
A catalogue record for this book is available from the British Library

ISBN: 978-1-138-21086-8 (Set)
ISBN: 978-1-315-40933-7 (Set) (ebk)
ISBN: 978-1-138-21708-9 (Volume 8) (hbk)
ISBN: 978-1-315-44152-8 (Volume 8) (ebk)

Publisher's Note
The publisher has gone to great lengths to ensure the quality of this reprint but points out that some imperfections in the original copies may be apparent.

Disclaimer
The publisher has made every effort to trace copyright holders and would welcome correspondence from those they have been unable to trace.

PROTECTIVE AND PREFERENTIAL IMPORT DUTIES

A. C. Pigou

Published in 1996 by

Routledge/Thoemmes Press
11 New Fetter Lane
London EC4P 4EE

in association with
The London School of Economics

This is a reprint of the first edition of 1906

Printed and bound in Great Britain by
Antony Rowe Ltd., Chippenham, Wiltshire

Routledge/Thoemmes Press is a joint imprint
of Routledge and Thoemmes Antiquarian Books Ltd.

British Library Cataloguing-in-Publication Data
A CIP record of this work is available from the British Library

Protective and Preferential Import Duties
ISBN 0-415-14391-8

Publisher's Note
The publisher has gone to great lengths to ensure the
quality of this reprint but points out that
some imperfections in the original may be apparent.

PROTECTIVE & PREFERENTIAL
IMPORT DUTIES

BY

A. C. PIGOU, M.A., F.S.S.

FELLOW OF KING'S COLLEGE, CAMBRIDGE

GIRDLER'S UNIVERSITY LECTURER IN ECONOMICS IN THE

UNIVERSITY OF CAMBRIDGE

AUTHOR OF 'THE PRINCIPLES AND METHODS OF INDUSTRIAL PEACE'

London

MACMILLAN AND CO., Limited

NEW YORK: THE MACMILLAN COMPANY

1906

EDITORIAL NOTE

This book was first published in 1906 and in recent years has been out of print. Messrs. Macmillan & Co., Ltd., the original publishers, have therefore generously granted permission for its inclusion in the present series. The editors wish also to acknowledge their indebtedness to the author, Professor Pigou, for equally readily granting his permission to reprint the work.

PREFACE

THE scope of this book is sufficiently indicated in the Introduction and in the Analytical Table of Contents. I am indebted to Messrs. Longman and the Editor of the *Edinburgh Review*, who have generously allowed me to make what use I wished of two articles contributed to their review in October 1904 and January 1906. I am under similar obligation to the Editor of the *Fortnightly Review* in respect of an article published by him in January 1904. Considerable portions of these articles are incorporated in various parts of this volume. On pages 16, 18-19, 73 and 109, citations are made, by permission, from my *Riddle of the Tariff*, published by Messrs. Brimley Johnson in 1903.

ANALYTICAL TABLE OF CONTENTS

INTRODUCTION

PART I

PROTECTIVE IMPORT DUTIES

CHAPTER I

PROTECTIVE DUTIES AND THE NATIONAL DIVIDEND

CHAPTER II

THE NATIONAL DIVIDEND AND THE NATIONAL WELFARE

PART II

PREFERENTIAL IMPORT DUTIES

CHAPTER I

THE DIRECT BUSINESS QUESTION

CHAPTER II

THE GENERAL QUESTION

§ 1. From what has been said it is evident that purely economic
investigation can do little to determine the practical issue.

INTRODUCTION

THE stimulus to the study of Economics is found now, as it has been in the past, chiefly in the bearing which that study has upon practice. But the meaning of "practice" has changed. In the days before Adam Smith the term signified almost exclusively the practice of the nation as a unit. Economics was valuable because it showed what the State ought to do in order to be strong and to maintain itself in the front rank of rival Powers. Now, however, it is understood that the scientific study of economic facts and causes may help to guide the policy not merely of the State, but also of private persons within it. Economics, in short, is seen to be relevant to the practice of individual "captains of industry" and voluntary associations of Co-operators and Trade Unionists as well as to that of the national Executive.

Associated with this point of difference there is a second. When the value of the science was thought to lie almost wholly in its political bearings, it was natural that what was written about it should be written in the form of party tracts. The "Economists" became a name for a political sect: so much so that Turgot distinguished himself from them upon the ground that he was not a monarchist. "Je ne suis point encyclopédiste, car je crois en Dieu ; je ne suis point économiste, car je ne voudrais pas de roi." Even Adam Smith's great work is not a scientific treatise in the sense in which that word would be used now, but is in large part a polemic against the dominant policy of Mercantilism. His attention is by no means confined to the tracing of causes and effects, but is extended to a vigorous explication of his views concerning good policy and bad. In this modern students have not followed him. Rather, they are coming to practise that doctrine of division of labour which their predecessors preached, and, at all events in their systematic works, to treat ethical and political argument as outside their special province.

This change of attitude is associated with a growing recognition of the fact that the part which economic conclusions should play in determining questions of practical politics is often exceedingly small. There are many things which a statesman has to consider besides the strictly business consequences of the measures which he passes into law. It is not an adequate argument in favour of any policy to say that the material prosperity, either of a class or even of the whole country, will be increased by it, nor is it an adequate argument against the policy to deny that economic proposition. To determine the goodness or the badness of a legislative proposal we need to balance the whole of its effects. Some of these will probably be economic ; others will not. Of the others the economist, as such, has no peculiar knowledge ; his science can tell him nothing, either of what they will be or, when their nature is given, of the relative importance belonging to them and to the economic effects proper. Whenever, therefore, he takes a side in a practical controversy, he must do this in virtue of his opinion upon many subjects concerning which he has no special means of forming a sound judgment.

This circumstance is important in two respects. On the one hand, it greatly weakens the authority of any consensus of economic experts in regard to a practical issue. But, on the other hand—and it is to this point that I wish to direct attention—it greatly mitigates the reproach to economic science that results from a disagreement of experts in regard to such an issue. It is often inferred from the conflict of view among distinguished authorities, which has become apparent in the course of the " fiscal controversy," that economic science itself is in a state of chaos, and that there are no principles generally recognised as true, This inference is not, I think, justified. I believe that between the leading controversialists on both sides —Professor Ashley, for example, on the one hand, and Professor Smart on the other—there is no disagreement on broad *economic* matters. Professor Ashley is well aware of the true relation between imports and exports. " Properly explained and qualified," he writes, " the proposition that in the long run exports must balance imports is a commonplace too evident for discussion." [1] Professor Smart is equally well aware that the absolute *a priori* method of advocating Free Trade, that does duty in much popular discussion, breaks down before serious analysis. It is not, of course, the fact that there is agreement upon all the theoretical points involved. That is not to be expected in any infant science. But there is a broad agreement.

[1] *Compatriots' Club Lecture* (First Series), p. 260.

For this reason, I am encouraged to hope, for the economic discussions which constitute the chief part of the following chapters, for some measure of acquiescence from those economists who favour a policy of Tariff Reform as well as from those who share my own views. The *answers* that I have given to the various questions raised, depending as they often do upon quantitative analysis and judgments of relative importance, are, of course, highly disputable. But, as to the *questions* which it is right to ask and the general form appropriate to an inquiry of this kind, it is time, I think, for us to acknowledge to one another that we stand upon common ground.

My book consists of two parts. The former deals broadly with the probable effects of moderate protective duties in a country such as England. In the first chapter I discuss their bearing upon the size of the National Dividend, and in the second the suggestion that, even though diminishing wealth, they may promote welfare. The latter part of the book is devoted to a detailed examination of the policy of Preferential Tariffs between the Mother Country and her Colonies, as it has been presented by Mr. Chamberlain. This part also is divided into two chapters, dealing respectively with the *Business Question* and the *General Question.*

NOTE.—The page references to List's *National System of Political Economy* refer to Lloyd's English translation, first edition ; those to Marshall's *Principles of Economics* to the fourth edition ; and those to Ashley's *Tariff Problem* to the first edition.

PART I

PROTECTIVE IMPORT DUTIES

CHAPTER I

§ 1. THE *National Dividend* in any year is the " net aggregate of commodities, material and immaterial, including services of all kinds," [1] available for consumption within the country. It is the product of the labour and capital of the people acting on the natural resources of their territory. These yield a large quantity of goods and services for direct consumption, and a smaller quantity to be sent abroad in exchange for other goods. The goods obtained by national production only and those obtained by national production *plus* international exchange are alike parts of the National Dividend.

To impede foreign trade is to prevent a number of people within the country from obtaining certain goods by the process of national production *plus* international exchange, and to force them to obtain them—or others —by that of national production alone. But, presumably, if people prefer the roundabout process, they expect, by resort to it, to obtain more of the goods they want for a given expenditure of productive power. No doubt, they may make mistakes or find themselves defrauded.

---

[1] Marshall, *Principles of Economics*, p. 594.

In certain classes of contract the probability of fraud may even be so great as to create a presumption that such contracts—payment by truck, for instance—ought not to be permitted at all. But, in general, what a person chooses as his immediate material interest is more likely really to be so than anything that a distant official, by means of a general rule, can hope to press upon him. Each person, therefore, if allowed to exchange as he will, may be expected to obtain a larger modicum of dividend than he would obtain if "managed" from above.[1] The National Dividend is, however, the sum of the private dividends of the members of the nation. Hence it follows that the dividend of the whole community is, *prima facie*, larger when exchange is free than when it is subjected to impediments.

§ 2. This general argument applies to all impediments to international (or, indeed, to any other kind of) trade. For closer study, however, it is necessary to make a double distinction within the broad class "impediments." First, they may be divided into those which do and those which do not impede the importation of goods that are capable of being made at home ; secondly, into those which do and those which do not

---

[1] The enlargement of the dividend does not, of course, necessarily take the form of an increase in the consumption of those commodities, in respect of which productive power has increased, proportionate to the increase of productive power. To speak quite accurately, "the direct and indirect benefit to a country from international trade is measured by the excess of the real value to her of the commodities which she imports over the real value to her of the commodities which, if foreign trade were cut off, she could and would make for herself with the capital and labour that she now expends upon making her exports and covering the expenses of her foreign trade." This description is borrowed from Professor Marshall.

yield a contribution to the national exchequer. Protective duties fall into the former division under each of these heads. They are impediments which do impede the importation of goods that are capable of being made at home, and they do (unless so high as to be prohibitive) yield a contribution to the national exchequer. The final question in regard to them, to which this chapter seeks an answer, is whether, when *all* their effects are taken into account, they are likely to make the National Dividend larger or smaller than some practicable means of raising an equal revenue. This question, however, cannot be attacked directly. For the *prima facie* argument against all impediments, explained in the last section, is often supposed to break down in the case of *protective* impediments, and it is held that these impediments in reality increase the National Dividend, apart altogether from their contribution to the exchequer. I shall therefore, in the first instance, examine this position.

§ 3. I may say at once that I am to a large extent in sympathy with it. The *prima facie* argument of my first section, so far as it refers to protective impediments, is, as will presently be shown, open to grave objections. Before, however, I pass to the valid and important arguments that are associated with the names, and derived from the works, of Hamilton and Friedrich List, it is desirable to notice an objection whose validity is more questionable. This objection is countenanced by Professor Ashley. It is to the effect that Protection may attract foreign capital, and, hence, indirectly increase the National Dividend by more than it directly lessens it. Thus, Professor Ashley writes : " Adam Smith argued that Protection could only divert capital from one industry to another; the Protectionists can reply that in many instances it has attracted fresh capital into the country ";[1] and he defends this view by citing a list of firms that have, as a matter of history, transplanted their works to some protected area.

It is here necessary to distinguish the question whether Protection really has the effect which Professor Ashley suggests from the different question whether his instances prove it to have this effect. To the second of these questions the answer is, I think, in the negative. The thesis is that the *net flow* of capital into a country is increased by Protective duties. It is impossible to prove this from the fact that certain specific pieces of capital are caused to flow into it. The opposing argument admits that fact, but contends that a greater sum of capital is caused to flow out of the country. Mr. Price, indeed, speaks of Professor Ashley's instances as "awkward facts" which furnish "contradictions" to the "absolute conclusions" of his opponents.[2] But, as I understand the matter, he has here misconceived the issue. Would it not be as pertinent to urge that a decrease in our import of beans "contradicts" the "absolute conclusion" that our imports as a whole have increased ? Indeed, Mr. Price may be invited to consider the thesis : " The awkward fact that the sea sometimes flows into rivers, contradicts the 'absolute conclusion' that rivers on the whole flow into the sea."

The circumstance, however, that Professor Ashley's instances do not prove his case does not suffice to *dis-*

[1] *The Tariff Problem*, p. 78.
[2] *Economic Review*, p. 334, July 1906.

prove it. The question must, therefore, be considered on its merits. The correct view appears to be as follows. Provided that, *apart from its effect* in attracting capital, Protection injures the National Dividend, it will probably lower the average real returns to capital in the country. Consequently, on the whole, the advantage to be obtained by foreign capitalists from investments there is likely to be diminished. It is, of course, *possible* that these foreigners may for some reason fail to act in accordance with their advantage. The presumption, however, is the other way. Consequently, except when Protection benefits a country apart from its influence on foreign capital, this influence is likely to prove repellent and not attractive to that capital.[1] The net flow is likely to be outward and not inward. The inward part will, indeed, be concentrated, and therefore seen, and the outward scattered and unseen, but this circumstance in no way conflicts with the view that the outward is the greater. A secondary effect on Capital cannot, therefore, be appealed to by those Protectionists who admit that the primary effect of Protection on the National Dividend is bad. A net inward flow cannot compensate other injuries, for a condition of its coming is that no compensation is required.[2] It gives only to them that have already, and takes away from them that have not. No reasoning, therefore, on Professor Ashley's lines, can reverse the *prima facie* conclusion of our first section,

---

[1] Cf. Professor Marshall's judgment on the effects of the M'Kinley Tariff (*Presidential Address to Section F of the British Association*, 1889).

[2] More strictly, the condition is that the injury to the general rate of interest must be *less* in the protected country than in the world in general.

that impediments to foreign trade are likely to lessen the National Dividend.

§ 4. I now pass to the great contention which Hamilton and List urged against the orthodox "Classical School." This school, enunciating the argument sketched in my first section, boldly took their stand by it as something absolute and final. Ricardo, for instance, asserted, in a quite unqualified manner, that, "under a system of perfectly free commerce, each country naturally devotes its capital and labour to such employments as are most beneficial to each."[1] List, on the other hand, rightly denied that this sweeping inference was warranted by the reasoning upon which it was founded. The classical analysis showed, indeed, that the direct and immediate effect of unimpeded foreign trade was to increase the National Dividend. But direct and immediate effects are not the sole effects. "The power of producing wealth is infinitely more important than wealth itself."[2] Consequently, "the nation must sacrifice and give up a measure of material prosperity in order to gain culture, skill, and powers of united production; *it must sacrifice some present advantage in order to insure to itself future ones*. . . . It is true that Protective duties at first increase the price of manufactured goods; but it is just as true, and moreover acknowledged by the prevailing economical school, that in the course of time, by the nation being enabled to build up a completely developed manufacturing power of its own, those goods are produced more cheaply at home than the price at which they can be imported from foreign parts."[3]

[1] *Political Economy*, p. 144.
[2] *A National System of Political Economy*, p. 133. [3] *Ibid*. p. 144-45.

When List wrote, England had established herself as the dominant manufacturing Power. He did not deny that, for the moment, continental nations would obtain the largest return to their capital and labour by buying from her. He was aware that at that time she could produce manufactured goods more easily than they could. But he was also aware that "the commodities which a country can now produce most easily" are not necessarily identical with those which it "has the greatest natural advantages for producing." For natural advantages require for their development time and exercise. The building up of manufacturing power, involving, as it does, the training of workmen, the perfecting of machinery, of transport, of credit, and of market organisation, may take years to accomplish.[1] Till it is completed, the old-established manufacturing State has "a thousand advantages over the newly-born or half-grown manufactories of other nations."[2] Consequently, if things are allowed to take their "natural course," the development of the latent powers of the younger states may be delayed for an indefinite period. In such a case the artificial exclusion of foreign goods may be the best possible policy.

Of the formal validity of List's argument there is no longer any dispute among economists. Granted that Protection involves an immediate detriment to the National Dividend, nobody supposes that it *must*, therefore, involve a detriment on the whole. On the contrary, the argument would now be stripped of the special reference to infant industries which List had chiefly in view, and be given a wider application. In

---

[1] Cf. *A National System of Political Economy*, p. 300.
[2] *Ibid.* p. 300.

its modern form, it would he stated somewhat in this wise. By stimulating the development or hindering the atrophy of productive powers, Protection may lead to an ultimate gain more than commensurate with the immediate loss. In short, a nation, like an individual, may be well advised, at certain stages of its history, to dispense with present wealth for the sake either of education or of insurance.

§ 5. The above conclusion is abstract and general. For practice we need to know, not only that the indirect benefit resulting from an impediment to foreign trade *may* outweigh the direct evil, but also in what circumstances that result is likely to be realised.

A part of the answer to this question is supplied by List himself. The main element of productive power, whose development involves a long process, is a population trained in the general atmosphere of industrial pursuits. If a country is entirely agricultural and has no important class of artisans or factory workers, the skill required for starting any particular kind of mill will be very difficult to get. "Masters, foremen, and workmen must first be either trained up at home or procured from abroad, and the profitableness of the business has not been sufficiently tested to give capitalists confidence in its success."[1] For a long time, therefore, it is improbable that any works which may be started will be able to compete on equal terms with established foreign rivals—and that in spite of the fact that the industry in question may be one for which the country has great natural advantages. On the other hand, in a country which is already

---

[1] *A National System of Political Economy*, p. 294.

largely industrial, the initial difficulty involved in starting a new industry is likely to be much slighter. For much less time is required to obtain from among a people already accustomed to many varieties of factory work, hands capable of carrying on a new variety of it. Further, in an industrial community, those other important elements of productive power, organised systems of transport and of credit, which, in an agricultural country, may need themselves to be built up before manufactures can be profitably established, are presumably already in existence.

From these considerations it follows that the case for Protection with a view to building up productive power is strong in any agricultural country which seems to possess natural advantages for manufacturing. In such a country the immediate loss arising from the check to the exchange of native produce for foreign manufactures may well be outweighed by the gain from the greater rapidity with which the home manufacturing power is developed. The "crutches to teach the new manufactures to walk," as Colbert called protective duties, may teach them this so much earlier than they would have learnt it, if left to themselves, that the cost of the crutches is more than repaid.

In a country, on the other hand, which is already industrial, the initial difficulty of starting a new industry in the face of foreign competition is, for the reasons just explained, much slighter. Therefore, so soon as it promises to be profitable, such an industry is almost certain to be started by private enterprise, without any artificial stimulus. Consequently, the probability that crutches would form a profitable investment is small.

The latter position is, of course, that occupied by our own country at the present time.

§ 6. The answer thus given to List's argument is, however, only a partial one.   For, as already indicated, the general principle of that argument extends far beyond the special case of infant industries.   The fact, therefore, that England is a developed industrial State does not, of itself, rebut the view that our industrial powers could be fortified by impediments to the import of foreign goods.   On the contrary, certain writers believe that Protection would help forward this result in two ways.   First, by making the market for our products *wider*, it would, they hold, enable manufacturers to increase the scale of their output, and so to secure various economies of production; secondly, by obviating the unfair attacks of foreign monopolists, it would prevent the destruction of industries naturally suited to this country.

§ 7. The plea for a wider market is based on the proposition that, in certain cases, an increase in the scale upon which a commodity is produced will diminish the average expenses of production.   Protection, it is said, would cause English manufacturers to supply practically the whole of the home demand, and also to gain a further footing in the foreign market by means of goods offered at reduced rates.   In this way they would be enabled to produce in enormous quantities, and so to introduce economies which are beyond the reach of smaller concerns.   Thus, there would result a real gain to the British consumer, because, though home-made goods would be sold more cheaply to the foreigner than to him, yet the prices demanded, even in this country, would be lower than they would have been except for the expansive influence of Protection upon the general organisation of industry.

Upon this argument, as thus interpreted, an important comment needs to be made. An "increase in the scale of production" may mean any one of four things : first, an increase in the aggregate quantity of the commodity produced in the country ; secondly, an increase in the average size of the individual plants producing it; thirdly, a closer approximation on the part of these plants towards producing up to their full capacity ; and, lastly, an increase in the area of production controlled, or number of plants managed, by a business of representative size.

Protection to any industry certainly means an increase in the scale of its production in the first of these four senses. But it is evident that a mere increase in the already enormous aggregate output of any of the staple goods manufactured in England could not inaugurate any appreciable economies. In order to this effect, an increase in the scale of production in one of the other senses distinguished above would also need to come about.

So far as the size of individual plants is concerned, it appears, however, that the effect must be very small. It can hardly be doubted that, with an aggregate output so great as ours, the point has already been reached, after which the size of the whole ceases to be a significant factor in determining that of the representative part. Protection would, of course, mean an increase in the number of factories, but scarcely in their average size.

Its effect in stimulating production up to full capacity, or, in other words, in diminishing short time,

C

and thus enabling the work to be done more economically,[1] is also likely to be unimportant. No doubt, the imposition of a new import duty would bring about a considerable *immediate* gain in this respect. But the advantage would not last; for, as the protected industry became more profitable, capital would be diverted into it and new works started. When time had been given for things to readjust themselves, the industry would, indeed, be larger, but there is no reason to suppose that the average amount of short time would be less than it is at present, and, therefore, no reason to anticipate any reduction of costs.

There remains the fourth sense of an increase in the scale of production—an enlargement of the area of production controlled by a representative employer. There are two forms of "integration of industry" by which this may come about: the vertical kind, where, as in the Carnegie Company, all the *successive processes* of a complex manufacture are co-ordinated under one management; and the horizontal kind, exemplified by the ordinary Trust, where a number of firms engaged upon the *same process* are united. The former kind of integration is the more favourable of the two to economies, and the less likely to lead to monopoly. There is, however, no evidence to show that it is especially likely to take place under a system of Protection. On the contrary, there have recently been several instances among firms engaged in the various branches of the British iron and steel trades in which it has come about, not merely without the assistance

---

[1] The Tariff Commission print some interesting figures to show the reduction in cost that may be obtained when full time is worked (*Report*, vol. i. §§ 55-6).

of that artificial stimulus, but under the direct influence
of the foreign competition which it would be the
purpose of Protection to restrict.

With the second kind of integration the case is
different. The Trust and the Kartel are believed by
the best authorities to be, in part at least, the product
of Protective Tariffs. From the former it is no doubt
true that economies in production and distribution
generally result; but the benefit of them almost
invariably accrues, not to the consumer, but to the
monopolistic corporation by which the market is
dominated. The Kartel, in general, is even more
pernicious than the Trust, since it is a mere monopoly
without the compensating advantage of a common
management. The fact that Protection tends to
promote the formation of bodies of this kind can
scarcely be used as an argument in favour of that
policy.

§ 8. I pass to the second respect in which List's
argument is thought to bear upon the actual conditions
of this country, the case, namely, of destructive
dumping. Clearly, if it may be desirable, at the
cost of the direct loss involved in impediments to
exchange, to build up manufacturing power, it may
also be desirable, at like cost, to defend that power,
when established, against destruction by hostile
attack. Furthermore, such hostile attack may occur.
It is conceivable that foreign combinations might
deliberately adopt a policy of killing British rivals
in order to establish an exclusive control over our
market. They might sell in England at low prices
—prices so low as to involve a positive loss—until
our industries were destroyed, and then, no longer

having any competitors to fear, might gather in the
fruit of their labours by raising prices to a very high
level.   In the face of action of that kind, to check
the import of their cheap goods, though still involving
a direct loss, might, nevertheless, be sound policy, as
tending to save us from monopolistic exactions after-
wards.   Of course, it would not necessarily be sound
policy even in that case; for, very often, the threatened
firms would be rich and strong enough to defend
themselves without direct or indirect governmental
aid.   Thus List, after he has argued that, in consequence of foreign aggression, "in a short time a
complex combination of productive powers and of
property becomes lost, which has been created only
by the exertions and endeavours of several generations," proceeds on the same page to point out that,
"when the Government is unable to provide any
remedy for its (*i.e.* an export trade's) interruption, we
often see manufacturers continuing to produce at an
actual loss.   They want to avert, in expectation of
better times, the irrecoverable injury which they would
suffer from a stoppage of their works."[1]   Still, the
formal validity of the above argument for State action
is not disputed.   The practical question is: Does
this kind of dumping, as a matter of fact, take place,
or is there any ground for supposing that it is likely
to do so?   So far as the facts go, there is no evidence
that anything of the kind has yet occurred.   It is
true, no doubt, that Mr. Brailsford and other " experts "
have stated that the Steel Kartel in the last few
years has pursued the policy just described.   But in
the official memorandum prepared for the Board of

---

[1] *A National System of Political Economy,* p. 298.

Trade precisely the opposite opinion is emphatically put forward :—

It is, of course, easy to suppose a state of things in which a Kartel, or a combination of Kartels, might deliberately export at a low price, with the principal or the exclusive aim of injuring, and ultimately of entirely ruining and bringing to a close, a particular industry in a foreign country. But it cannot be said that there is any clear evidence of such action on the part of the German combinations, whose export policy up to the present time appears to be mainly the result of supply exceeding demand in the German domestic markets.[1]

I am not, be it observed, maintaining that destructive dumping does not exist at all. On the contrary, it certainly exists in the home market of Protectionist, and sometimes even of Free Trade, countries. There are plenty of cases in which American Trusts have " dumped " goods in the markets of native competitors, in order to ruin those competitors and maintain their own monopoly. There have been instances of the same thing even in England. A Birmingham concern, for example, engaged in the manufacture of screws, is popularly supposed, at one period, to have succeeded in dumping other English screw-makers out of existence. But destructive dumping into England from abroad does

[1] Cd. 1761, p. 298. It is sometimes argued *a priori* that destructive dumping *must* take place, since some foreign goods are sold here more cheaply than in the country of origin. The conclusion does not follow, for, as the Tariff Commissioners rightly observe (*Report*, § 61), a policy of two prices may be directly profitable to those who pursue it without reference to ulterior results. No arguments can be framed for Protection against goods imported in pursuance of that policy other than those which are applicable to Protection in general.

not take place, and for a very simple reason. The only purpose of that policy is to secure the control of the supply, and therewith the power to exact monopoly prices. In the native market, especially in a protected country, where the competition of foreign imports is hindered by a tariff, there is no reason why that result should not be achieved; but, in the British market, if a German Kartel or an American Trust kills British competitors, what advantage has it ? It is still prevented from reaping its reward by the presence of sellers from other foreign countries. It will not, therefore, be worth its while to "dump" unless it has not merely an American or a German, but a world-embracing monopoly. It is conceivable that, some day, that danger may arise, and that, when it does, the least inconvenient way of meeting it may be by means of an import duty. Hitherto, however, there is no indication of its approach, and those who know the difficulty of forming and maintaining Kartel arrangements covering wide areas will be very sceptical when dolorous prophecies concerning it are made.

§ 9. From these considerations it appears that, though circumstances *may* exist in which Protection would *ultimately* benefit the National Dividend, there is no reason to suppose that such circumstances *do* exist in England at the present time. Since, therefore, the argument of our first section proves that Protection must *immediately* injure the dividend, we conclude that it is likely to injure it on the whole. I pass, therefore, to the different and more difficult question whether the collection of a given revenue by duties of a protective character is likely to injure the dividend more than the collection of an equal revenue in some other way. The alternative with which I shall compare these duties in the first instance is a customs duty accompanied by a corresponding excise duty upon home production.

§ 10. Economists are agreed that a part of the direct burden of *import* duties is, in general, shifted permanently on to foreigners. I am not referring to the fact that, for a short time after the imposition of a new import duty, *the foreign producer of the taxed article* is forced to make a contribution to the revenue of the taxing country, and to put up with lower returns than those received in other similar occupations in his own country. This circumstance is essentially transitory. Capital and labour will begin to flow into the injured industry at a less rapid rate than before, until equilibrium is re-established and the return yielded by similar industries is again similar. Except, therefore, for a comparatively short period, no part of the burden of our tax can fall specifically and exclusively upon the foreign producers of the taxed article. When we have to deal with duties intended to be lasting, that particular kind of extraneous contribution need not, therefore, be taken into account. The way in which a part of the burden of a duty is *pe manently* thrown abroad is different. The particular industry whose product we tax must, in the long run, yield the same return as other foreign industries, *but our taxation will have had the effect of slightly reducing the real return of all foreign industries.* It will have altered the rate of interchange in our favour, and so compelled the generality of foreign consumers to offer a little more than before of their products in exchange for a given quantity of ours. In other words, it will have led to a slight rise in the prices of British exports abroad, and a slight fall in the prices of foreign imports in England. In this indirect way the foreigner is forced to contribute permanently to our National Dividend of goods and services.

It thus appears that, *other things equal*, it is better for a country to raise a given revenue by import (or export) duties than by any other kind of commodity tax. Even if the contribution thus secured from foreigners is small, it is larger than could be secured in any other way. Thus, if there were two *different* commodities, the conditions of demand and supply of, and the aggregate expenditure upon, which were exactly similar, and if one were produced at home and the other imported, it would be better to raise revenue from the imported than from the native product. In both cases the loss of money and of surplus to consumers of the taxed commodity would be the same. But, if the foreign commodity were taxed, the real cost of other foreign articles would be indirectly lowered, whereas, if the home commodity were taxed, no such result would follow. There is, therefore, a presumption in favour of raising revenue by means of import duties.

The above consideration clearly affords an argument in favour of import duties as contrasted with any form of internal taxation yielding an equal revenue. As between different kinds of import duties, the presumption is that the foreigner's contribution will be larger, the larger the amount of revenue raised upon the processes of international trade. For, the larger the impediment thus imposed, the more are our takings from the world in general (as valued apart from the tax) likely to be diminished; and, the more these takings are diminished, the greater is the alteration in the ratio of interchange. Since, however, a protective import duty yielding a million pounds involves the levying of a million on the processes of foreign trade, while a customs *plus* excise duty upon the same commodity, assessed to yield an equal revenue, involves the levying of a smaller sum upon these processes, it follows that the foreigner's contribution is likely to be larger under the plan of a protective import duty. The gain to the National Dividend would, no doubt, be slight. For, in view of the presence of competing sellers in our foreign markets, and the consequent large elasticity of the foreign demand for our goods, a given alteration in our takings from abroad would alter the ratio of interchange by a much smaller percentage than that by which our takings had altered. Still, it is probable that there would be *some* advantage. The real cost of our foreign imports, other than the one taxed, would be slightly lowered, and we should obtain a larger quantity of them for the same expenditure of industrial energy.

§ 11. This indirect influence is not, however, the chief element that has to be considered. Account must also be taken of the direct gain and loss in respect of the taxed article itself. This aspect of the problem is best approached through the general theory of differential taxation.

When a commodity is supplied to any market from two separate sources, any revenue that may be required can be raised either by a relatively high duty on the supply from one, or by a relatively low duty on that from both of those sources. The question I propose is, Which of these two methods is directly the more advantageous to the taxing authority?

Let us begin with the simple case in which both sources of supply are foreign. It is then clear that, from the standpoint of the taxing country, that form of duty is the better which has the smaller effect upon price; for, the less price rises, the smaller is the amount by which consumption, or, in other words, the National Dividend in respect of the taxed commodity, contracts.[1]

Now, it is popularly supposed that, in this regard, a differential duty is necessarily and always inferior to a non-differential duty; for does it not divert productive power from its natural channels and thereby lessen its efficiency? This opinion is plausible, but it is incorrect. No doubt, as I have already said, in order to yield a given revenue, a higher rate of duty is required when a part than when the whole of the supply is taxed. But, on the other hand, under the differential system, owing to the competition of the untaxed sources, the price would rise by a smaller proportion of the tax than it would do under the other system. These two considerations point in opposite directions, and it is not obvious under which plan the absolute price change would be the greater.

This question can, however, be determined. The solution is that a differential duty raises price more

---

[1] The greater this contraction, the greater, of course, is the loss of consumer's surplus in respect of that part of the consumption which would have taken place apart from the tax, but, by its operation, is destroyed.

than a non-differential duty yielding an equal revenue, *only* if the supply from the taxed source is more elastic than that from the other, and therefore than that from both together, or if, being less elastic, its defect of elasticity falls short of a given small amount. This proposition, while only vaguely commending itself to unaided reflection, can be established by mathematical analysis.[1] Hence it follows that, from

---

[1] Elasticity is measured by the proportion in which a given proportionate change in price alters the quantity supplied or demanded.

Let A and B be the quantities supplied in the two sources and π the price in the absence of any tax.

Let e_1, e_2, η be the elasticities of supply and demand involved.

Let R be the revenue required.

Let T_1, T_2 be the rates of duty required to yield this revenue when one source (*i.e.* A) or both sources respectively are taxed, and let $\Delta\pi_1$, $\Delta\pi_2$ be the corresponding increases of price.

Let both sources obey the law of diminishing return, and let both T_1 and T_2 be small relatively to π.

It is easily proved, as a first approximation, that

$$\frac{\Delta\pi_2}{\Delta\pi_1} = \frac{e_1A + e_2B}{e_1A} \frac{T_2}{T_1}.$$

Therefore the price rises more when both sources are taxed if

$$T_2 > \frac{e_1A}{e_1A + e_2B} T_1.$$

We know that

$$R = T_1A\left\{1 + e_1\frac{\Delta\pi_1 - T_1}{\pi}\right\}$$

$$= T_1A\left\{1 - e_1\frac{e_2B - \eta(A+B)}{e_1A + e_2B - \eta(A+B)} \frac{T_1}{\pi}\right\}.$$

Similarly

$$R = T_2\left[A\left\{1 - e_1\frac{-\eta(A+B)}{e_1A + e_2B - \eta(A+B)} \frac{T_2}{\pi}\right\}\right.$$
$$\left. + B\left\{1 - e_2\frac{-\eta(A+B)}{e_1A + e_2B - \eta(A+B)} \frac{T_2}{\pi}\right\}\right].$$

$$\therefore T_2^2\left\{\frac{\eta(A+B)(e_1A + e_2B)}{\pi\{e_1A + e_2B - \eta(A+B)\}}\right\} + T_2(A+B)$$
$$- \left[T_1A - T_1^2\frac{e_1\{e_2B - \eta(A+B)\}A}{\pi(e_1A + e_2B - \eta(A+B))}\right] = 0.$$

the standpoint of the National Dividend, there is a presumption in favour of raising revenue by differential

The problem is to find under what conditions the root of this equation when solved for $T_2 > < \dfrac{e_1A}{e_1A + e_2B}T_1$.

The equation may be written

$$-pT_2^2 + qT_2 - H = 0$$

where p and q and H are all positive quantities.

Consequently, it has two positive roots; and it can be proved that, if a given value γ be substituted in the left-hand branch of the equation, and if the resulting expression be positive, then γ must be > the smaller root of the equation. If the resulting expression is negative, γ must be < the smaller root of the equation. It is with the smaller root alone that we are concerned, since it may be assumed that the least possible tax capable of raising the revenue required will be imposed.

Hence, we have merely to substitute $T_1\dfrac{e_1A}{e_1A + e_2B}$ for T_2 in the left-hand branch of the above equation. If the result be positive, $T_2 < \dfrac{e_1A}{e_1A + e_2B}T_1$, and, therefore, the price falls when both sources are taxed instead of one; if it is negative, the reverse is the case.

Substituting, and writing $\{e_1A + e_2B - \eta(A + B)\} = K$, we get

$$T_1^2\frac{1}{\pi K}.\left\{\frac{\eta(A+B)(e_1A)^2}{e_1A+e_2B} + c_1A\{e_2B - \eta(A+B)\}\right\} + T_1\left\{\frac{e_1A(A+B)}{e_1A+e_2B} - A\right\}$$

$$= \frac{T_1}{e_1A+e_2B}\left[\frac{T_1}{\pi.\ K}\left(\eta(A+B)\{(e_1A)^2 - (e_1A)^2 - e_1Ae_2B.\}\right.\right.$$
$$\left.\left. + e_1A.\ c_2B(e_1A+e_2B)\right) + AB(e_1 - e_2)\right].$$

This is positive if the following expression is positive, namely

$$\frac{T_1}{\pi K}.\left\{e_1A.\ e_2B\{-\eta(A+B) + e_1A + e_2B\}\right\} + AB(e_1 - e_2)$$

$$= \frac{T_1}{\pi}\left\{e_1A.\ e_2B\right\} + AB(e_1 - e_2) = AB\left\{e_1e_2\frac{T_1}{\pi} + e_1 - e_2\right\}.$$

This expression is positive if

$$e_1 > e_2\frac{1}{1 + \left\{\dfrac{T_1}{\pi}e_2\right\}}.$$

Under these conditions, therefore,

$$T_2 < \frac{e_1A}{e_1A + e_2B}T_1, \text{ and therefore } \Delta\pi_2 < \Delta\pi_1.$$

duties assessed upon one source, provided that that source is considerably less elastic than the other.

It thus becomes important to inquire whether the foreign supply of goods imported into England is likely to be less elastic than the home supply. In special cases the answer is certainly in the affirmative. When there is a surplus in some foreign country of a commodity for which England is the only available large dumping-ground, it will pay the foreign manufacturer to accept what price he can get, and the amount of his sales will scarcely be altered by the imposition of a tax at our ports. Special duties upon dumped surplus would, therefore, be an excellent means to revenue. If moderate in amount, they would replenish the exchequer without much affecting the price paid by consumers. In theory there is here some scope for national gain. In practice, however, as will be argued in the next chapter, it would be easy for intending dumpers to evade the trap laid for them, and so to deprive us of our expected *coup*.[1]

The case of foreign goods imported in the ordinary way is different. Here the presumption is that the domestic supply is the less elastic of the two. For, presuming, as in the absence of knowledge is reasonable, that the elasticity of *production* is the same at home and abroad, the elasticity of the home supply will be equal to, but that of the foreign supply to our

In other words, under these conditions the price falls when both sources are taxed instead of one.

Hence the price is raised less when the given revenue is collected from both sources, than when it is collected from the more elastic source, or from the less elastic source if its elasticity falls short of that of the other by less than a defined small proportion.

[1] Cf. *post*, pp. 73-4.

market more, than this. The reason is that a given rise of price in England will increase the *proportion* of the foreign production that comes to us as well as the aggregate amount of that production.[1] Consequently, in the general case, as regards the circumstances of the taxed article itself, the presumption is adverse to the imposition of protective duties as contrasted with import *plus* excise duties upon the same commodity. This presumption has to be set against the opposite presumption in favour of protective duties, which was seen to arise from their relation to the ratio of international interchange. The latter presumption appears to depend on an estimate of quantities of a lower order of magnitude than those involved in the former, and is, therefore, in general outweighed.

§ 12. There remains, however, a further consideration of great importance. In the case of protective duties, unlike that of duties differentiating between two foreign sources of supply, the consumers in whom the taxing authority is interested are themselves also the producers in one of the sources of supply. Consequently, the protective duty, *cetèris paribus*, has this advantage over the customs *plus* excise duty. When it is imposed, a part of the burden inflicted upon con-sumers is not a net burden to the country, but is a mere transfer of wealth to other persons in the country.

---

[1] Let A be the foreign production, and D the foreign consumption. Let e be the elasticity of production, both in England and abroad, and η that of the foreign demand.

Then, for a given rise of price in the English market, the foreign import rises from $(A - D)$ by $(eA - \eta D)$.

Therefore, the elasticity of the foreign supply to our market is $\dfrac{eA - \eta D}{A - D}$. Since η is negative, this is $> e$.

Thus, suppose that the sources of supply are of similar elasticity, and that, therefore, the rise of price and consequent burden to consumers is nearly equal under the two plans. The burden to the country is then not equal. On the contrary, it is less under the protective duty by the rise of price under that duty multiplied by rather more than the old home production, *plus* the fall of price to producers which would have resulted under the customs *plus* excise duty, multiplied by rather less than the old home production.

It does not follow from this that protective import duties are necessarily better than customs *plus* excise duties.[1] When the elasticity of supply of the foreign goods is not smaller by the required amount, the more extensive rise of price and consequent greater burden to consumers has to be balanced against the advantage just distinguished. Which of these is likely to be the greater it is impossible to say without detailed investigation in each case.

§ 13. A comparison between protective import duties and import duties, like those on tea and sugar, which are not protective because levied on non-competing commodities, can be conducted on similar lines. First, since both kinds of duties impose the

---

[1] It is only where all second powers can be neglected, including the loss of the consumer's surplus on that part of the consumption which the tax destroys, that the direct burden under a protective, can be proved smaller than that under a customs *plus* excise, duty.

If R be the revenue required, A the supply from the taxed, B from the untaxed source, and e_a, e_b, η the elasticities of supply and demand respectively, the direct advantage of the latter over the former plan is, under these circumstances, measured by

$$R\left\{\frac{e_b B}{e_a A + e_b B - \eta(A + B)}\right\}.$$

same monetary impediment upon foreign trade, there is no presumption that the protective duty will affect the ratio of international interchange more favourably than the other. Secondly, the presumption against the protective duty drawn from the probable greater elasticity of foreign as compared with home supplies disappears; for both the supplies concerned are foreign. Lastly, the presumption in favour of protective duties derived from the fact that part of the burden they inflict upon consumers is balanced by a corresponding gain to producers within the country is somewhat weakened. For the non-protective import duty does not, like the customs *plus* excise duty, inflict a burden upon these producers—a burden which constitutes an addition to the relative advantage of a protective duty.

§ 14. On the whole, therefore, import duties on non-competing commodities are not conspicuously better or worse than customs *plus* excise duties, and the relation of moderate protective duties to both of them is much the same as their relation to one another. In fact, there is no general *a priori* presumption either for or against the imposition of protective duties as a means to raising revenue. In pure theory we cannot say whether they are likely to make the National Dividend larger or smaller than it would be if the same revenue were collected from import duties of a non-protective character. Any proposed protective duty must, therefore, be examined in detail, and contrasted with a specific alternative. *Prima facie* it is as likely to be beneficial as to be injurious to the National Dividend.

§ 15. This conclusion is, of course, very different

from the sweeping condemnation with which popular
Free Trade theory envelops all proposals in any way
tainted with Protection.   It is, however, necessary to
guard against ambiguity.   My argument has shown
that a moderate protective import duty upon a commodity selected at random is no more likely to injure
the National Dividend than a non-protective import
duty designed to yield the same revenue and assessed
on a non-competing commodity also selected at random.
But this is not the comparison which current practical
proposals require that we should make.   Our present
non-protective import duties are selected, not at
random, but with a special view to their fitness as a
means to revenue.   The duties contemplated by the
Tariff Commission and numerous politicians are also
not to be selected at random.   The motive underlying
their selection, however, is the very opposite of fitness
to yield a revenue.   It is fitness to exclude goods that
compete with British labour.   Duties levied upon that
plan are, from the nature of the case, likely to be
bad as revenue duties; for, the more completely they
protect the home producer, the smaller, of necessity,
is the revenue they yield.   Our practical choice,
therefore, really lies between non-protective duties
chosen for their merits, and protective duties chosen,
one might almost say, for their demerits, as engines of
revenue.   Our willingness to substitute a random protective for a random non-protective duty cannot carry
approval of a policy such as this.   If it were introduced the National Dividend would almost entirely
be reduced.

§ 16. It is, no doubt, *possible* that this result might
be obviated were a protective tariff to prove itself a

D

potent instrument for bargaining with foreign countries. It is often urged that, if armed with such a tariff, we should have something to concede in fiscal negotiation, and could, therefore, obtain greater advantages for our goods in the markets of the world. This view is compatible with the fact that we already enjoy most - favoured - nation treatment in all important respects, and could in no case hope for preferential treatment from foreign countries. For, though there is nominally no discrimination against British goods, and though the taxes levied upon any particular class of them, in Germany for example, are identical with those levied upon the same goods when they are imported from elsewhere, yet there may be a real adverse discrimination in the class of goods which foreigners elect to tax ; and it is possible that, with greater bargaining power, we might get rid of this discrimination, or even substitute for it a new discrimination favourable to ourselves. If we succeeded in doing this, it is *possible* that the National Dividend would be increased indirectly by more than it was directly diminished.

Whether a result of this kind is *probable* is a political more than an economic question. The answer to it depends chiefly upon the skill of our own negotiators and the complacency of those of other countries. It is, however, important to make the question itself precise. What we have to compare is not, on the one hand, the National Dividend as diminished by the direct action of a protective tariff and augmented by its indirect action in facilitating bargaining, and, on the other hand, that same dividend undiminished by a protective tariff and not augmented by any bargaining. To state the question in that way is to imply that, in the absence of a protective tariff, bargaining is impossible. But that is not the case. Non-protective duties may also serve as instruments of negotiation. Sir Louis Mallet, for example, was of opinion that much might be effected, without any departure from our Free Trade policy, by friendly representations, backed, at need, by small manipulations of the purely revenue duties on wine and tobacco.[1] Furthermore, even if protective duties were imposed on occasions, as weapons of war, this would not necessarily imply—in theory at least—the regular establishment of a protective tariff. On the whole, therefore, though it is probable that, by maintaining such a tariff *and bargaining with it*, we should obtain better terms abroad than by not maintaining it and not bargaining, it is by no means equally probable that the terms we should obtain in this way would be better than those secured by not maintaining the tariff, and bargaining with other instruments. At all events, the gain to the National Dividend through the *difference* between the terms in these two cases is almost certain to be slight. In my judgment, it would probably fall far short of the loss induced by the direct operation of a protective tariff itself.[2]

[1] *Memoir of Sir Louis Mallet*, p. 104.

[2] On the general question of Tariff Bargaining, cf. my *Riddle of the Tariff*, chap. iv. A more elaborate discussion is contained in Professor Dietzel's excellent *Vergeltungszölle*, recently translated into English.

CHAPTER II

§ 1. THE conclusion reached in the preceding chapter is not decisive. It has been shown that any general scheme of protective duties, selected with a view to their protective effect, would almost certainly injure the National Dividend more severely than the collection of an equal revenue by means of non-protective duties. But this is not enough. *Prima facie*, no doubt, anything that enlarges the dividend is likely to be advantageous, and anything that diminishes it, disadvantageous to the country as a whole. But these results are not certain. For the welfare of the whole is not dependent merely upon the wealth of the whole. It is also dependent upon other circumstances,[1] and it is possible that a policy which lessened the size of the dividend might, at the same time, affect these circumstances so favourably that welfare on the whole would be increased.

[1] It is dependent, for instance, *inter alia*, on the desirableness of desired satisfactions and of the desires which these satisfactions stimulate. The welfare of China might, for instance, be promoted by a subtraction from its national dividend of all the opium it now consumes. This class of consideration has no special bearing upon foreign trade as such. Nobody denies that it may be well to prohibit some foreign goods—and some domestic goods—upon moral grounds.

§ 2. Among these circumstances perhaps the most important is the way in which the National Dividend is distributed. This point has been seized in recent discussions, and some controversialists, realising its significance, have set themselves to show that a protective system, even if it were to lessen the aggregate dividend of the country, would, nevertheless, improve the fortunes of the labouring classes. Thus, Mr. Chamberlain in a speech at Birmingham declared : " Year by year the balance of trade gets greater and greater against us. Who is it that loses by this ? Is it the rich ? Not necessarily at all. They may continue to make more money than ever—by financial operations, by carrying their works abroad, and by other devices. The people who lose are the working people of this country. . . . The working man, and the working man alone, is the sufferer." [1]

To some it might seem that this reasoning should be brushed aside as irrelevant to political practice. The business of the Government, it might be said, is to forward the general interest of the whole community and not to concern itself with the special interest of a part. In confirmation of this view, the financial ideals of Mr. Gladstone might be cited. " We have been steadily endeavouring," that statesman declared on one occasion, " to extricate ourselves from the vicious habit of looking to the supposed claims and supposed separate and rival interests of classes, and to legislate simply and exclusively for the interest of the country at large. . . . I believe that legislation for the benefit of a class is a mistake of the first order. . . . It is a betrayal of our duty to the nation, whose trustees we are without

[1] Mr. Chamberlain at Birmingham, *Times*, Nov. 4, 1905.

distinction of class." [1]   Eloquent and impressive, however, as this passage undoubtedly is, any demurrer to
our reasoning founded upon it is altogether beside the
point.   It is certainly the duty of statesmen to consider the interests of the whole, but those interests are
not necessarily advanced by an augmentation of the
National Dividend, if this augmentation involves a
change of distribution unfavourable to the poor.   It is
clear, for instance, that a community need not become
more prosperous if its rich men add a million pounds
to their incomes at a cost of, say, half a million of
wages to the labouring population.   Consequently,
Mr. Chamberlain's contention is not irrelevant, but
demands careful investigation.   The arguments commonly employed in support of it are twofold, partly
statistical, partly economic.   These I shall pass in
review before submitting the conclusions at which I
have myself arrived.

§ 3. There are two ways in which, if adequate data
were available, statistical reasoning could be employed.
First, figures indicative of the condition of the working
classes at any given period might be collected for a
number of Free Trade countries, and similar statistics
for a number of Protectionist countries.   If the
countries selected were sufficiently numerous, if the
fiscal policy pursued in each were not a *result* of the
industrial conditions prevailing there, and if any given
policy could be assumed to act in the same sense under
all industrial conditions, a comparison of the statistics
thus obtained would be an application of the method
of difference, and would show *a posteriori* whether
Free Trade or Protection were economically the more

---

[1] Quoted by Sydney Buxton, *Finance and Politics*, i. p. 347.

advantageous to the interests of the working classes. Secondly, statistics indicative of *changes* in the condition of these classes might be collected over a series of years for a number of countries, with a view to showing, on the same lines as before, whether their prosperity increased more rapidly under Free Trade or under Protection.

It may be said at once that there are no sufficient data for an application of either of these methods. Neither Protectionist nor Free Trade countries are numerous enough to warrant resort to it. In the few of them for which statistics are available, general conditions are so various that the fortunes and progress of the working classes would differ enormously whatever fiscal policy were adopted. Naïvely to attribute differences in the figures to differences in policy is to neglect the elements of statistical science.

This general reasoning is by itself decisive, and, from the standpoint of a scientific discussion, does not need detailed support. So much stress, however, has recently been laid by advocates of "Tariff Reform" upon the case of Germany that their appeal to the circumstances of that country cannot be wholly ignored. This appeal involves a comparison both of existing conditions there and here and of recent rates of progress in the two countries.

The argument by absolute comparison was worked out in leaflet No. 88 of the Imperial Tariff Committee (President, Mr. Chamberlain). "In 1903 the number of emigrants for every 10,000 of the population was in England thirty-five, in Germany six. In 1903 the percentage of unemployed in trade unions was in England 5·3, in Germany 2·3. The amount, per head of population, in savings banks is in England £4 : 11s., in Germany £7 : 17s." The implied inference is that the Protectionist policy of Germany is better for the working man than the Free Trade policy of England.

Prima facie the reasoning seems persuasive. Since, however, statistics are susceptible of manipulation, caution suggests that we should trace those figures to their origin. That task is, fortunately, an easy one. In 1904 the Board of Trade published an important Blue-book [Cd. 2337], entitled *British and Foreign Trade and Industry* (Second Series). This Blue-book deals with all the points mentioned in the leaflet, and is cited by the writer as one of the sources from which he drew his information. A comparison of the source with the stream that filters through his hands yields some interesting results.

The statistics of emigration quoted in the leaflet have the best show of justification. The following comments are, however, relevant. (1) For the " United Kingdom " of the Blue-book, " England " has been substituted in the leaflet. (2) The Blue-book shows that our emigration rate in 1903 (35 per 10,000) exceeded that of the previous year by more than ten, and that of any other year subsequent to 1894 by more than fifteen ; in the leaflet these facts are suppressed. (3) The Blue-book shows that, of the recent increase in the rate, by far the greater part has been due to emigration to outlying portions of our own Empire, and that in 1903 the destination of nineteen out of every thirty-five emigrants was British ; this fact is suppressed. (4) In the Blue-book we read : " Still less is it an easy task to institute international comparisons, the basis on which the emigration statistics are compiled in different countries being far from uniform." [1]   This also is suppressed.

The second figure in the leaflet refers to savings banks.   In this case the deception is more serious. On the first page of the section of the Blue-book headed " Savings Bank Deposits in the Principal Countries," the following passage occurs :

An attempt may be made to compare working-class savings in different countries by a comparison of the statistics of savings banks, co-operative and friendly societies, and other similar institutions.   Such comparisons, however, are usually unsatisfactory for the following reasons, among others :

1. There are no data enabling a comparison to be made of the total deposits in *all* institutions in which working men deposit their savings.

2.   Even if such data were available, we should not know, for each country, what proportion of the total deposits represents savings of classes other than the working class.

3. If we confine our comparison to a single class of institution, *e.g.* savings banks, it is vitiated by the fact that the conditions of deposit, *e.g.* maximum limit of deposit, rate of interest, etc., differ in different countries, and the degrees to which savings banks are exposed to the competition of other modes of thrift and other classes of provident institutions also vary very greatly.

It follows that savings banks are likely to be attractive to working-class savings and to the savings of other classes in different degrees in different countries, so that there will be no uniformity either as regards the extent to which the total deposits in these banks are representative of the whole savings of the working classes, or as regards the proportion of these deposits which are drawn from other than working-class sources. [2]

[1] [Cd. 2337] p. 159.   [2] *Ibid.* p. 174.

The third figure quoted concerns unemployment. Here, again, the leaflet suppresses an essential fact. The Blue-book section on "Unemployed Statistics in Foreign Countries" (p. 104) opens with this passage:

It may be said at once that no unemployed statistics exist in any foreign country on a basis which allows a comparison to be made of the actual level of employment in that country and the United Kingdom respectively at a given time.

The method of the leaflet is illumined by the further fact that in France, also a Protectionist country, the unemployed figure for 1903 was 10·1. This figure, at least as comparable with ours as the German one, is suppressed. Further comment is scarcely required.

Rem facias ; rem,
Si possis, recte ; si non, quocumque modo rem !

So far of the precise figures contained in the leaflet. In addition to these there is the more vague statement: "The cost of living on the whole is *not higher* in Germany than in England. Butter, pork, eggs, milk, potatoes and other vegetables, beer, spirits, and tobacco are all cheaper in Germany." The following comments may be made. (1) At the beginning of the section in the Blue-book, in which statistics under most of the above heads are cited, we read:

Comparisons of absolute prices of commodities in different countries are far more difficult than comparisons of rates of change of such prices, inasmuch as we have to be sure that the qualities of the articles compared are approximately the same. In some cases this is impossible; in other cases it would yield a misleading result, seeing that the staple articles most usually consumed in the different countries may not be identical in quality. With these reservations the following figures are given.[1]

In the leaflet this caution is suppressed. (2) In the Blue-book, comparative figures are given for the important commodities flour and sugar, indicating that both are decidedly more expensive in Germany than in England. These commodities are not mentioned in the leaflet. (3) Taking all the articles of food, for which the Blue-book gives figures, and weighting them equally, we find that the geometric mean of their prices is 6 per cent higher in England than in Germany; when rice and sugar are omitted, it is 17 per cent higher. On the other hand, it is stated in the same Blue-book, as " the most probable result from our present imperfect data," that the average level in money of industrial wages in Germany is two-thirds of that in the United Kingdom.[2] If this conclusion, which is not mentioned in the leaflet, is combined with the foregoing price statistics, it appears that the level of *real* industrial wages in this country must exceed the German level by a quarter or a fifth. I do not claim for this result any positive value. It seems, however, to show that the argument from a comparison of *existing conditions* in England and Germany, if it could be permitted as an argument at all, would not work out in the way that Tariff Reformers pretend.

The argument from the comparative *progress* of

---

[1] [Cd. 1761] p. 221.

[2] *Ibid.* p. 290. It is probably right to add to the German wage the compulsory contribution to workmen's insurance on the part of employers. This contribution is, however, too small to affect the argument. It is put by Professor Ashley at "about 2 per cent additional wages" (*Progress of the German Working Classes*, p. 18).

England and Germany frequently occurs in Mr. Chamberlain's speeches. At Bristol he expressed it thus :

> In Germany, take that as an instance . . . wages have increased in greater proportion than here. Emigration has diminished enormously. It is not diminishing in anything like the same proportion—indeed, it has not practically diminished at all—in England. The savings of the people have multiplied in a much larger degree. The cost of living has diminished there as well as here.[1]

The statement that the emigration rate has declined more rapidly in Germany is true. Down to 1894 the curves for the two countries moved similarly, and, since that date, the German curve has fallen considerably below the English. In the Board of Trade inquiry [2] various reasons for this change are suggested. I am absolved, however, from going into the matter by the fact that the immediate antecedent of the new movement was a considerable diminution of Protection in Germany, brought about by the Caprivi treaties of the early nineties. It can scarcely be argued that an improvement, which began when Protection was made less stringent, is *prima facie* itself the result of Protection.

The statement that the savings of the people have multiplied much faster in Germany is unwarranted. The deposits in savings banks per head of the population did, indeed, increase between 1880 and 1890 by some 86 per cent in that country as against 30 per cent in England. Between 1890 and 1900, however, the percentage growth has been practically the same

---

[1] *Times*, Nov. 22, 1905.   [2] [Cd. 2337] p. 166.

in the two countries.[1]   Furthermore, as already
observed, it is dangerous to infer from savings banks
deposits to savings in general, since large masses of
savings are invested in other institutions, for which
comparative figures are lacking.

The statement that wages have increased in greater
proportion in Germany, coupled with the remark that
the cost of living has diminished there as well as here,
misrepresents the facts.   Both assertions are literally
true; but they conceal the conclusion, to which the
figures apparently point, that real wages have risen
faster here.   From the Blue-book [Cd. 1761] it
appears that since 1886, the first year for which
comparative statistics are available, industrial wages
in terms of money have moved as follows, the wages
for 1886-90 being represented for each country
by 100 :—

TABLE I

Changes in Industrial Wages in terms of money

	United Kingdom.	Germany.
1886-1890 . .	100	100
1891-1895 . .	105·5	105
1896-1900 . .	110·3	113·9

The above table takes account of money wages
only.   Table II., printed below, takes account of the
movement of prices as well as of the wage movement,
and thus measures fluctuations in terms, not of money,
but of the things that money can buy.   It is reached

[1] [Cd. 2337] p. 195.

by combining the table just given with Table P,
headed "Changes in average level of retail prices of
food to a workman's family in Germany and United
Kingdom" in the first fiscal Blue-book.[1]

TABLE II

	United Kingdom.	Germany.
1886-1890　. .	100	100
1891-1895　. .	109·6	100·8
1896-1900　. .	119·9	113·9

The second Blue-book fails to bring up to date the
figures upon which Table I. is based. Consequently,
neither table can be carried beyond the year 1900.
It should be noted that Table II. corrects for prices
of food only, there being no figures for the other
items that enter into a workman's weekly budget.
So far as any conclusion is warranted by these imperfect data, it is that the statistics of money wages
have masked the real relative movement in England
and Germany, and that, as a matter of fact, our own
workmen have been progressing at a more, and not
at a less, rapid rate than their continental neighbours.
As in the case of comparative conditions, so in that of
comparative progress, I submit no positive argument.
In the present state of knowledge, trustworthy statistical treatment of the problem along either of these
lines seems to me wholly impracticable.[2]

[1] [Cd. 1761] p. 224.
[2] In this view I may claim the energetic support of Professor
Ashley. Cf. *Progress of the German Working Classes*, passim,

§ 4. I now turn from the statistical to the economic side of the popular argument. Mr. Chamberlain's speeches may again serve for a text. The working classes, he declares, "lose when those [*i.e.* foreign] countries are allowed to send more manufactures to us,"[1] because, when this occurs, work is taken abroad which might otherwise have been done in England; with the result that industries, capable of employing a great number of men, are contracted, or possibly even destroyed. This reasoning, persuasive enough in itself, is reinforced by instances, taken from the town in which the orator happens to be speaking, of specific local industries that have suffered from the effects of foreign competition. In the face of these things it is not difficult to understand that many admirable and sympathetic men regard free imports as the main cause of unemployment and Protection as the infallible cure.

There is, however, a serious logical gap in all this. Nobody denies that foreign competition with any particular British industry tends to contract the scope of that industry, and, hence, the aggregate of wages annually expended in it. That this must happen is, indeed, too obvious for argument. Nor is it less obvious that protection to an industry, everything else remaining the same, would expand that industry and

especially p. 2 : "It requires but little reflection to understand why it is that a direct comparison, exceedingly difficult and insecure as it must be in the case of any two countries, is absolutely valueless as applied to Germany and Great Britain." In the face of this and many similar passages it is interesting to note that the writer of leaflet No. 88 mentions Professor Ashley's book as one of his authorities.

[1] Mr. Chamberlain at Birmingham, *Times*, Nov. 4, 1905.

augment its wages-bill. A tariff on imported steel
means, *ceteris paribus*, more money spent on steel-
making in England. That is a primary *datum* that
nobody can possibly dispute. The contention on the
other side is, not that protection to steel will fail to
benefit steel-makers, but that it will fail to benefit
them so much as it injures the workpeople in other
industries. The direct stimulating effect on the
favoured trade is, indeed, the more palpable. It is
concentrated at one point and is, therefore, plainly
visible. The indirect depressing effect, on the other
hand, is spread over a great number of industries and
is, therefore, concealed. It is as though a sluice were
opened between a large reservoir and a small one.
The volume of water in the large reservoir might be
lessened more than that in the small one was increased,
but in the latter the change would be obvious, in the
former scarcely noticeable.

Whatever may be thought of the inherent value of
this Free Trade contention, it is at least clear that no
amount of declamation concerning the direct benefits
of Protection can afford an answer to it. These effects
are admitted; the argument is that the indirect effects
outweigh them. To answer this argument by repeating
that the direct effects exist is to be guilty of an
ignoratio elenchi. Even, therefore, if the Protectionist
conclusion is correct, it is in no way demonstrated by
the Protectionist argument. The economic considerations popularly advanced are, in fact, as inadequate to
that end as the statistical considerations examined in
the preceding section.

§ 5. Popular argument may now be left aside, and
the question whether Protection would be likely to

benefit the poor approached directly. The investigation must be pursued mainly by the analytic method; for direct arguments from history are always charged with, and often guilty of, the fallacy *post hoc, ergo propter hoc*. Nevertheless, in view of the widespread misconceptions that prevail, it will be well to establish certain matters of fact.

First : during the past forty years there has occurred an enormous increase in our imports of wholly and mainly manufactured goods, and there has also occurred an enormous improvement in the general circumstances of the labouring classes. On the one hand, wholly and mainly manufactured imports have increased from an average of £31,000,000 in 1860-64 to £131,000,000 in 1900-1903. On the other hand, according to estimates prepared by Mr. A. L. Bowley, the total amount paid in wages has risen from some £300,000,000 to some £700,000,000, in spite of the fact that Sauerbeck's index number of wholesale prices has fallen nearly 30 per cent.[1] The increase of population during the period has been 23 per cent.

Secondly : the general average percentage of workmen returned as unemployed by Trade Unions has remained fairly constant. It has neither increased with the great rise in manufactured imports, nor diminished with the great rise in wages.

Thirdly : fluctuations in wage rates, pauperism, and the percentage of Trade Unionists out of work are closely correlated, wages and pauperism tending to lag in their movement one year behind employment. This fact is brought out in the diagram that follows.

[1] *Economic Journal*, Sept. 1904, p. 459.

E

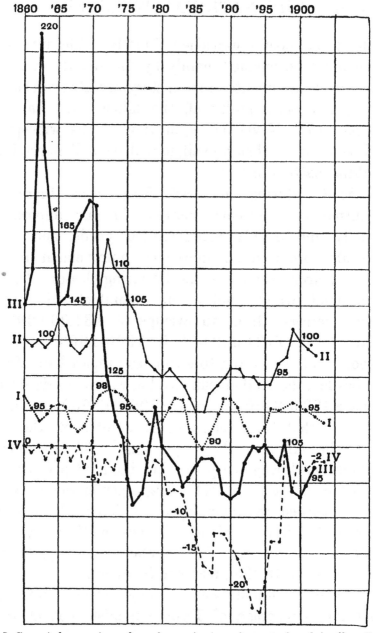

I. Corrected percentage of members not returned as out of work in all available Trade Unions.

II. Index of deviations from the trend in the general course of money-wages in the United Kingdom.

III. Mean number in thousands of able-bodied adult paupers in England and Wales.

IV. Index of deviations from the trend in imports of wholly and partly manufactured articles.

NOTE.—In curves I. and IV. the point on the curve under any year represents the facts of that year ; in II. and III. it represents those of the *succeeding* year.

The curve of wages is based on the index number published by Mr. A. L. Bowley in the *Economic Journal*.[1] This index number differs from that given in the Board of Trade Blue-book of the previous year, fluctuating, indeed, in a similar manner, but exhibiting a more decided upward trend. The reason for the divergence is that Mr. Bowley's figures do, and the Board of Trade's do not, allow for the changes that have taken place in the relative importance of different occupations. An allowance of this kind certainly ought to be made, and, therefore, Mr. Bowley's table is the better of the two.

The curve of employment is based, not on Mr. Bowley's figures, but on those worked out in the second Fiscal Blue-book (December 1904). In the tables there drawn up by the Board of Trade, account seems to have been taken of important materials not accessible to Mr. Bowley earlier in the year. The curve represents the computed average percentage of members of Trade Unions who were *not* returned as out of work at the end of each month in the years 1860-1903.[2]

The curve of pauperism is based on the statistics of able-bodied adult paupers, exclusive of vagrants, in England and Wales, published by the Board of Trade.[3]

The method of construction of the curves is as follows. Those for employment and pauperism are translated direct from the tables in the Blue-book. They represent simply the annual percentage of Trade Union members not returned as out of work, and the

[1] *Economic Journal*, Sept. 1904, p. 459.
[2] [Cd. 2337] p. 83.   [3] [Cd. 1761] p. 468.

absolute annual numbers of able-bodied paupers in
the several unions from 1860 onwards. In the
construction of the wages curve, however, a more
complex plan has been followed. Mr. Bowley's table
of wage index numbers has a strong general upward
trend. If our curve had been constructed directly
from this table, the deviations from the trend would
have been partially masked by the trend itself. It
is, however, with the deviations and not with the
general trend that our present purpose lies. In order,
therefore, that these may be properly exhibited, the
curve has been tipped into a horizontal position.
For exact tipping a large amount of arithmetical labour
would have been necessary. Consequently, the following device has been adopted. In Mr. Bowley's wage
table the trend is treated as roughly equivalent to a
series, whose value stands at 100 for the year 1901,
and diminishes by unity for each preceding year.
The curve in the diagram is found by adding to
Mr. Bowley's actual index number for each year the
difference between 100 and the figure for the trend
in that year.

Of the curves thus constructed, that for employment represents, under the year 1860, the figure for
1860, and similarly for succeeding years; the curves
for wages and pauperism represent, under 1860, the
figures for 1861, and so on throughout.

The diagram thus obtained shows, in the first
instance, a close positive correlation between movements of wage rate and employment respectively.
In almost every case an upward or downward movement in the one is accompanied by a similar movement
in the other. In like manner, both these curves are

negatively correlated with (*i.e.* move in the opposite direction to) the curve of pauperism.[1]

Fourthly : fluctuations in wage rate and the percentage of Trade Unionists out of work are not correlated positively, and fluctuations in pauperism are not correlated negatively, with fluctuations in manufactured imports. On the contrary, there is an appearance of correlation in the opposite sense.

This point also is brought out in the diagram. Below the curves of wages, employment, and pauperism, I have printed a fourth curve, described as an index of deviations from the trend in imports of wholly and mainly manufactured goods. This curve is based on the table given in [Cd. 2337],[2] and is constructed in a manner similar to that employed for the wages curve. It represents the series of differences between the actual imports and a trend of imports beginning at £26,000,000 in 1860, and increasing by one-tenth of that amount in each succeeding year. The reason for the adoption of this device for tipping the curve is, as in the case of the wages curve, to prevent deviations from the trend being masked by the trend itself. When this curve is compared with

[1] The relation which thus appears between the statistics of pauperism and of employment among Trade Unionists gives ground for increased confidence in the latter as indices of changes of employment in general. Directly, of course, the employment figures refer only to employment among Trade Unionists. Since, however, the services of unorganised labour are, in most industries, in some relation of direct or indirect dependence upon those of skilled men, it is commonly believed that the Union figures, though not perhaps indicative of the absolute amount of general unemployment at any time, afford trustworthy information of the direction in which this amount changes. The movement of the pauperism curve lends support to this opinion.   [2] P. 83.

the other three, it is at once apparent that there is
no general tendency on its part to move in the
opposite direction to the wages and employment
curves, or in the same direction as the pauperism
curve.   The only point at which such a tendency is
in any way suggested is about the year 1871, and
the movement there is readily explained by the
Franco-German war.   Nor is this all.   On closer
observation it appears that, from the time of that war
onwards, there is a distinct, if not very close, positive
correlation of curve IV. with I. and II. and a corresponding negative correlation with curve III.   Observe
especially the period beginning with 1881.   The
relative decline in manufactured imports that culminated
in 1887 is accompanied by a similar decline both in
employment and in wages.   The improvement that
followed is marked in all three curves, and so is the
decline of the early nineties.   The same remark holds
good of the recovery that followed.   The curves continue together till the outbreak of the Boer War.   In
all these cases the pauperism curve moves in the
opposite sense to the import curve.

Lastly, the great increase of manufactured imports
has not been accompanied by any increase in the
extent of the fluctuations that occur in the percentage
of Trade Unionists out of work.   This is readily seen
by inspection of the employment curve in the diagram.
In the middle period the curve seems to have been less
steady than in the early period; but in the later period
it returned again to the early form.[1]

[1] This point can, if necessary, be proved more exactly.   Of the
several measures of stability familiar to statisticians, the simplest is
the "mean deviation from the average."   Applying that measure to

These points are put forward as facts merely. They may serve as a corrective of popular misstatements, but they afford no proof either of the wisdom of Free Trade or of the unwisdom of any other fiscal policy. I pass, therefore, to analysis.

§ 6. In a group among whose members mobility is complete, it is easily shown that the interest of the whole and of the parts is harmonious. Imagine, for example, a community consisting exclusively of workmen, able to pass without friction from any one trade to any other. If the Government of that group puts a duty on imported boots, the immediate result is a gain to the bootmakers and a loss to everybody else. This result, however, cannot continue. For the boom in boots will attract labour into that industry and divert it from other industries, until a common level is again established. There will be a short period of transition, but things will soon settle down, and, when they have done so, no one division of the group can be affected differently from any other. Consequently, if the import duty lessens the dividend of the whole group, it necessarily lessens that of every part.

compare steadiness of employment as between the successive periods from 1860 that comprise entire wave-lengths from maximum to maximum, we obtain from the annual figures :

	Mean deviation from average.			Mean deviation from average.
[1860-64	1·40]		1882-88	2·48
1865-71	1·89		1889-98	1·67
1872-81	2·16		[1899-1903	·93]

The first and last of these figures are enclosed in square brackets, because they do not refer to complete wave-lengths.

It should be noted that in this calculation attention has been confined to *annual* percentages of employment. If it were worth while, the monthly figures, so far as available, could be treated in the same way.

Now, of course, in real life mobility within the different groups of industrial agents is not complete. Even unskilled labour cannot turn indifferently from one occupation to another. Still less can a skilled sugar-refiner transform himself into an iron-puddler, or a commercial traveller adopt the rôle of littérateur. Within the realm of capital, plant erected for gasworks cannot convert into a motor factory, or the machinery of a cotton mill be turned to the making of guns. Between the various uses of land similar barriers subsist. The conversion of arable into pasture land, or of pasture into building sites, is not a wholly frictionless operation. Within each of these industrial groups mobility does, indeed, exist, but it is hampered by serious impediments.

From the standpoint of the moment these considerations are fundamental. Since, however, Protection is never advocated except as a more or less lasting policy, this standpoint is not an appropriate one from which to examine it. For such a purpose we need to take a fairly long view of society, and, when we do this, the impediments to mobility that have been noticed no longer seem important. The factors of production present themselves, not as a stock, but as a flow. Within each broad group, the members, sprung, as it were, from a common ancestry, are differentiated into separate divisions under the stress of profit and loss. As a group flows into being from year to year, these divisions come to be tenanted in such relative proportions that the " attractiveness " of any one of them is equal to that of any other. It is thus that fresh accumulations of capital, new generations of workers, even established acres of soil, are silently pointed their road. The forces of equilibration are always at work. Though halting, they are continuous; and though, as with a viscous fluid in connected tanks, the tendency to a common level may, to the spectator of a moment, seem to make little way, for the far-sighted it is the great dominant factor, and all the impediments minor incidents. In the long-run, therefore, mobility is complete, and the interest of the whole cannot clash with that of any part.

The above argument applies broadly to any group consisting of a single industrial agent. It does not, however, apply to those great nation-groups in which a variety of such agents are embraced. For, as between one agent and another, the equilibrating force of mobility is much less conspicuous. When labour is depressed, no " run " seems long enough to allow it to transfer itself to landowning or capitalism. Is not the better view that the great divisions of the industrial world, land, capital, brain-labour, trained hand-labour, muscular labour, are non-competing, in the sense that, against those who would pass from one to another, there is a great gulf fixed ?[1]

From the standpoint of a very long period this view is not, indeed, accurate. In nature there are no hard lines, and correct analysis depicts competing character, not as rigidly present or absent, but as more or less present according to the relations of the object, and the length of the period, we are considering. Conclusions based on the assumption of immobility as between groups of industrial agents are thus necessarily imperfect. On the other hand, however, those suggested by the opposite assumption would be more imperfect still;

[1] Cf. Edgeworth, *Economic Journal,* 'xi. 587.

they would be vitiated throughout by the interaction of temporary earnings and permanent efficiency. The truth is that our problem is too complex for exact treatment, and that, in starting from the assumption of immobility, we are merely preferring a less to a greater inaccuracy. Fortunately, whatever error is thereby introduced tells against, and not in favour of, the thesis I am endeavouring to maintain.

Mobility absent, the interests of the whole and part are no longer necessarily harmonious. The appropriate analysis is as follows. Throughout the whole range of industry the "law of substitution" prevails. Employers tend to substitute one kind of labour or machine for another until the return from the last sovereign invested in each is the same. Between employers themselves the same law is at work. As a consequence, the National Dividend is distributed among the various factors of production in proportion to their marginal efficiencies. So long as the ratio between these remains unaltered, anything that increases the whole dividend necessarily adds to the share of each factor. Protective duties, however, besides affecting the dividend, may also change relative. efficiencies. They develop one manufacture, A, at the expense of another, B, and a given factor may play a more important part in the former than in the latter of these. In such a case that factor rises in marginal efficiency relatively to the others, and, consequently, secures a greater proportionate share of the National Dividend. The point is easily illustrated. Suppose, for example, that all agricultural imports into Great Britain were subjected to heavy taxation. Much of our industrial energy would thereupon be diverted from manufactures to agriculture. But the function of agricultural land is more important in the latter than in the former industry. Consequently, the marginal efficiency of agricultural land, relatively to that of capital and labour, and, hence, the proportion of the National Dividend accruing to agricultural landowners would be increased. In corresponding circumstances a like result would emerge in regard to any other factor of production. Nor need the gain achieved be merely proportional. The increase per cent in the share of the dividend obtained by the favoured factor might exceed the shrinkage per cent in the dividend itself. In that case, protective duties would involve an absolute, and not merely a relative, gain to that factor.

This is the judgment of pure theory. Since, however, in that sphere, almost anything can be proved *possible*, practice is little helped. What we really need to know is the *probability* of such a result occurring in England at the present time. On that point the following considerations may be submitted. First, we do not know that the part played by Labour in the industrial life fostered by Protection would, as a matter of fact, be any more important relatively to other factors than the part played by it now. So far as the evidence goes, it is just as likely to be less important. Secondly, if it is more important in any degree, Labour's *proportion* of the dividend would, indeed, be augmented ; but a *great* increase of importance would be needed to increase its *absolute quantum* —and it is this alone that matters. Thirdly, as between England and the rest of the world, capital is exceedingly mobile. If, therefore, the earnings of

Capital here are diminished — and, with the whole dividend reduced and the slice of it taken by Labour augmented, this can scarcely fail to happen—Capital would flow abroad in large quantities.[1] That movement would both react unfavourably on the aggregate dividend and also compel Labour to surrender to capitalists a larger proportion of what remained. Even, therefore, if Labour were to gain for the moment, it could scarcely retain its advantage. Fourthly—and this is my final point—even though it were true that Protection benefited *Labour*, it would not follow that it benefited *labouring people*. For labouring people are not mere embodiments of the factor Labour. They are also themselves capitalists, whose savings are not unimportant. No doubt, as Lord Goschen warns us in his admirable study of the *Growth of Moderate Incomes*, the available statistics must be used with caution. Part of the investments in savings banks belong to the children of the well-to-do, and there are other qualifications of a similar character. No matter, however, what stress is laid on these points, the general drift of the figures is highly significant.

In 1903 the number of depositors in Trustee and Post Office savings banks in the United Kingdom was 11,000,000, the deposits per head £17 : 18s., and the aggregate deposits £198,000,000. The number of members of industrial and provident (co-operative) societies was 2,000,000, the amount of share capital per member nearly £13, and the aggregate share capital

---

[1] There would probably also be a tendency for some of the remaining capital to seek investment in men rather than in machines, and this, so far, would be good. An argument on those lines, however, if adequate in favour of protective duties, is still more adequate for prohibiting mechanical inventions.

over £26,500,000. The number of building societies (a frequent form of investment for the poor) was 2062, and the liabilities £51,000,000.

Industrial companies (the insurance companies of the poor) had on their books (in 1904) 22,500,000 policies, aggregating £221,000,000, and averaging £9 : 16 : 5 per head. The membership of *ordinary* friendly societies was in 1902, the latest year for which statistics are accessible, 5,500,000, and the aggregated capital £36,500,000. The membership of *all classes* of friendly societies was 13,250,000, and the funds £45,000,000.

The membership of all trade unions was (1903) 1,900,000; for the hundred principal unions the income in 1903 was £2,000,000, and the funds in hand at the end of the year £4,500,000.[1]

In the face of such figures it is incorrect to treat the working classes as dependent merely on labour. Their stake in capital is also appreciable. Even, therefore, if it were proved that Protection would benefit labour, it does not follow that it would benefit labouring people. For, the dividend as a whole being reduced, capital would probably lose more than labour gained, and the capital of the poor would suffer with the rest. Solidarity might be wanting between factors of production, but might still exist between concrete classes. That the factor labour should gain through a policy injurious to the National Dividend I have already shown to be improbable; that the class "labouring people" should so gain is more improbable still.

[1] Cf. "Tenth Abstract of Labour Statistics of the United Kingdom, 1902-1904."

§ 7. There is, however, yet another way in which Protection might conceivably increase welfare even though its direct effect were to diminish both the National Dividend as a whole and the share of it that falls to the poor. It might alter the *manner* in which the labouring classes receive their share; and the alteration might be of such a kind as to react favourably upon character and *morale*. Thus, if the new policy were to lessen either (1) the proportion of people engaged in sweated industries, or (2) the transitions of industry, or (3) the irregularity of employment, the consequent improvement in the men might be well worth purchasing even at the cost of some reduction in their earnings. We have, therefore, to inquire whether it is likely to do any or all of these things.

§ 8. The first point has been raised in the following form. The trend of our export trade is, it is said, away from "staple" and towards "miscellaneous" industries—jam, pickles, slop clothing, furniture, and so forth. Consequently, the trend of employment is turned in the same direction, with the result that, between the last two censuses, the numbers employed in tailoring and furniture-making have increased much more rapidly than those engaged in staple industries. But the former group of industries are worked under worse conditions than the latter. Hence it follows that foreign trade is causing more people to work under bad conditions, with deleterious results both to physique and to character. It is, therefore, desirable that the nature of that trade should be modified, and that, instead of making slops with which to purchase staples, we should make the staples for ourselves.

This argument has been employed by Professor Ashley.[1] We need not inquire how far his view of the conditions of labour in the miscellaneous industries is complete. He himself has admitted that a considerable proportion of the tailoring industry is carried on in well-appointed modern factories, and it is unnecessary to remind him of the existence of Port Sunlight. Let it be granted that the facts are substantially as he has described them. It is sufficient to ask whether protection to British staples would be an adequate or a desirable remedy.

In the first place, it may be observed that tailoring and furniture-making are not the only expanding employments. Railway work, transport of all kinds, building, general and local Government service, commerce, trading, literature have all grown considerably between the last two censuses. Much of the work in these occupations is of a better class and carried on under better conditions than the bulk of that performed in cotton mills or iron works. If, then, we begin protecting these staples, what guarantee have we that men will be drawn up into them from below rather than down into them from above? Why, for instance, should a check imposed upon steel imports transfer labour to British steel works from "sweating dens" rather than from high-grade machine shops? Both effects would perhaps be produced to some slight extent. But, in view of the general sacrifice of material wealth which some advocates of this argument are ready to concede, it appears highly improbable that the good result would be so great as the bad.

[1] *The Tariff Problem*, pp. 106-110.

Furthermore, even supposing that Professor Ashley's remedy would do more good than harm, it does not follow that it ought in practice to be adopted. For there is a way at once simpler and more certain. It is difficult to see why bad conditions in the "miscellaneous" industries should be attacked by a remedy different from that which has been adopted in regard to all the other regulated industries of the country. When the operatives in cotton mills were oppressed and degraded as no workpeople are degraded now, the solution of the difficulty was not found in a tariff upon agricultural imports. It was found in factory legislation, inspection, and sanitary regulations—in protection, in short, not to goods but to men. If the conditions of the miscellaneous industries require a remedy, let them be dealt with along these well-tried lines. Let us, by all means, introduce additional workshop rules and more stringent methods of inspection; but let us avoid attempting, by a dubious and roundabout device, to remedy an evil which, experience shows, can be overthrown by direct assault. Professor Ashley's discussion may, perhaps, suggest the wisdom of further regulation of the conditions of industry; it can in no case sustain a plea for Governmental restrictions upon imported goods.

§ 9. The second point concerns the transitions of industry. The ordinary economic argument against Protection ignores, it is said, the loss involved in the process of change from one industry to another. When English consumers begin to purchase foreign bicycles, and, consequently, transform their old demand for English bicycles into a new demand for exportable blankets, wherewith to purchase bicycles, the change is not accomplished instantaneously and without friction. On the contrary, whenever it comes about, it is accompanied by a heavy sacrifice of human quality. I am not referring now to the permanent consequences of temporary unemployment while new work is being sought. Those I reserve to the next section. The point here is that the men who are forced out of the old industry, even when they have found new work, are likely to have lost the earning power that used to belong to their acquired skill, and, consequently, to stand in an inferior occupation and on a lower plane of wages. The result may be a degradation of their habits, and a lowering of the whole tone of life, not merely for themselves, but, what is more important, for the children dependent upon them.

Considerations of this order appeal strongly to men of humane sentiments, and naturally suggest to them a demand for State action to prevent the transitions from which such evils spring. A careful scrutiny of the facts, however, does much to mitigate the justice of their plea.

In the first place, industrial transitions and the ill consequences that follow them are by no means confined to industries in which foreign competition plays an important part. Dislocation of industry through this cause is, in fact, only a single species of a large genus, and there is no reason to suppose that the transitions involved in it are in general more injurious than other transitions. Indeed, since the disturbances resulting from mechanical inventions are often sudden, while those due to the development of international trade are usually gradual, it would seem that the latter are likely, if anything, to be less injurious.

Hence, we ought not to condemn international trade on account of the transitions involved in it, unless we are at the same time prepared to condemn mechanical inventions.

But, in the second place, the amount of evil involved in all kinds of transitions is much exaggerated by popular opinion. These are but rarely accomplished in a violent and ruinous manner. They do not in a moment eject a hundred thousand workmen from the employment to which they are trained. That is not the way in which the industrial organism accomplishes its changes. Rather, the returns in a particular class of business begin to fall; as old plant becomes worn out, it is only partially, or not at all, replaced; the wages to be made in that occupation drop a little relatively to those prevalent in others, or, perhaps, the employment available at the old wage somewhat declines; consequently, workpeople less readily put their children to that trade, and the flow of labour into it is checked. A small number of men who have been trained to the trade may, no doubt, be driven to sacrifice their skill and to pass over into some new occupation. That *many* would find it necessary to do this is not, however, to be expected. Such at least is the teaching of recent English experience as interpreted by Mr. Bowley. Discussing the shifting of population in England over the last three censuses, he writes:

The main changes may have been accomplished, so far as the broad figures show, without any necessity on the part of any man to change his occupation, but simply by changes in the supply of new-comers. If a proportion of lads bred in the country had gone to the railways and coal mines and taken situations as bus-drivers, grooms, or gardeners, and if the lads in Yorkshire and Lancashire, whose fathers were in the woollen and cotton mills, had gone into the cycle or machine trades or ship-building, or become clerks in the cities, the numbers would have grouped themselves very much as the census shows. It seems very probable that such changes have taken place. The only case, numerically important, where there is an actual diminution of numbers is agriculture, and this would be sufficiently accounted for by the non-filling of the places of the old men as they dropped out of the ranks.[1]

Furthermore, even in those cases where a change of trade among adults really does occur, the loss of skill under the modern system will generally be small. The training received in one kind of factory is often of great service in another. As Professor Marshall explains: " Manual skill that is so specialised that it is quite incapable of being transferred from one occupation to another is becoming steadily a less and less important factor in production." [2]   In view of all this, the circumstances would need to be unusual under which the community would lose more by the process, than it would gain from the fact, of transition. For, after all, the evils of the process necessarily last only a short time ; whereas the benefits of the fact may be permanent.[3]   There is, therefore, a strong presumption that the aggregated effects of the change and the changing would be good.   It is still arguable, no doubt, that the State should in some way smooth

---

[1] *National Progress in Wealth and Trade*, pp. 1, 2.

[2] *Principles of Economics*, p. 286.

[3] Where the fact of change is the result of a manipulation of foreign tariffs, and is likely to be reversed in the near future by a manipulation in the opposite sense, the case is somewhat different. But foreign countries are not, as a matter of fact, continually moving their tariffs up and down in this way.

the path of the individuals who suffer from a process thus conducive to the general advantage, but scarcely arguable that, for their sake, it should interdict the process itself.

§ 10. A much more important point is the effect of Protection upon, first, the average amount, and, secondly, the fluctuations, of "employment" among men willing to work. Under this head the difficulties both of analysis and of exposition are serious. For "employment" itself is an ambiguous term. I say nothing of the difficulties that arise when attempts are made to measure it intensively and not merely extensively by the time occupied. The point rather is that "employment" is used for the opposite, sometimes of "unemployment," if such a word may be permitted, and sometimes of "the unemployed." Now, so far as *fluctuations* of employment are concerned, this ambiguity does not matter. For, first, irregularity of employment in either sense carries with it irregularity of earnings, and is, therefore, a palpable evil;[1] and, secondly, fluctuations in "unemployment" and in the number of the "unemployed" naturally take place at

---

[1] Cf. Foxwell : " I cannot venture to say what would be the general opinion of the working classes on the point ; but my own feeling would be that, when a certain necessary limit had been reached, regularity of income was far more important than amount of income. Where employment is precarious, thrift and self-reliance are discouraged. The savings of years may be swallowed up in a few months. A fatalistic spirit is developed. Where all is uncertain and there is not much to lose, reckless over-population is certain to set in. . . . The working class suffers most. To this class thrift and prudence are absolutely vital ; and it emerges from a period of disturbance with its standard of comfort seriously lowered, and with a corresponding loss of social position " (*The Claims of Labour*, p. 196).

the same time and in the same direction. The case, however, is otherwise with the *average amount* of employment. On the one hand, the aggregate earnings of labour being taken as fixed, a small amount of employment in the sense of short hours and numerous holidays is a great gain to Labour. On the other hand, a small amount of it in the sense of many men involuntarily without a job is a great evil; it means in practice, not that everybody, from time to time, gets a few days' "playing," but that, while good workmen are in pretty continuous work, the inferior men in the various industries are chronically on the streets for long periods together.[1]

There are, thus, three distinct questions. First, how does Protection affect "employment" in the sense of the aggregate quantum of work that has to be done for given earnings; secondly, how does it affect the average number of men out of a job; thirdly, how does it affect the fluctuations that occur about this latter average?

The first of these questions need not detain us. If, in accordance with previous reasoning, Protection lessens both the National Dividend as a whole, and that slice of it that goes to Labour, the hours of work are apt to be longer and not shorter than they would otherwise have been. The very fact that wages are

---

[1] This point is illustrated by the analysis of time lost by work-people through unemployment in the Amalgamated Society of Engineers from 1887 to 1895 (published in Cd. 2337). The results show "that, taking good and bad years together, about 70·4 per cent of the whole number of members lost less than three working days per annum through want of work; 13 per cent lost between three days and four weeks; 4·6 per cent from four to eight weeks; 2·8 per cent from eight to twelve weeks; and the remainder, about 9 per cent of the whole, lost over 12 weeks" ([Cd. 2337] p. 99).

low necessitates long hours as a means to subsistence earnings. It is a commonplace that hours of labour decline as wages rise, and that they tend to be lowest among the most prosperous sections of the working classes. Protection is likely to increase employment in the sense of exacting more work for the same real wage and lessening the labourer's time of leisure.

The second question is more complex. The average proportion of men out of work depends upon two main causes. In the first place, it cannot be isolated from the general policy pursued by Labour in the matter of wages. So far as custom fixes a rigid minimum, forbidding the older or less competent workmen to accept lower rates than their companions, it makes it less easy for them to secure employment. The proportion of men out of work is thus a function of the workpeople's wage-policy. So far as it depends upon this, it has nothing to do with the fiscal system that happens to be in vogue.

In the second place, the average proportion out of work depends in part upon the stability of industry. Much of the enforced idleness that exists is due to the fact that the industrial machine is in a state of motion. Wants change with fashion, means of supplying wants with new inventions and developing transport. Labour and capital strive continually to adapt themselves to this varying process. But they are not mobile or far-sighted enough to adapt themselves completely. Maladjustments occur both in space and time. Supply follows hard on the heels of demand, but lacks the speed to overtake it. Hence, there is necessarily a fringe of men in movement. They are at once a means by which adjustment is sought, and a proof that it is not found. The average number unemployed from this cause varies with what may be called the organisation of mobility, with the development, that is to say, of agencies for moving people, spreading information, and cultivating foresight.[1] So far it is clearly unconnected with fiscal policy. But the average number unemployed depends also on the nature of the particulars from which the average is derived. In those trades where the variations in these are largest, the average itself is also largest.[2] The variations, however, depend upon the stability of industry, and that in turn partly depends upon fiscal policy. At this point, therefore, for the first time, Protection and the Unemployed come into connection. If Protection makes for stability, it lessens the average number of persons out of work as well as the fluctuations about that average.

Hence, our second and third questions reduce themselves to one. Under both heads, Protection is beneficial if it steadies, injurious if it disturbs, industry. Nor is this all. The National Dividend itself is not, as has been tacitly supposed hitherto, determined independently of the extent to which industry fluctuates. Fluctuations mean the periodic idleness of certain productive resources, and hence, *ceteris paribus*, make the dividend less than it would otherwise be. Consequently, if it could be proved that Protection made for stability, the case against it from the standpoint of Labour would be weakened in three distinct ways.

[1] As Professor Marshall puts it : "The constancy of employment depends on the organisation of industry and trade, and on the success with which those who arrange supply are able to forecast coming movements of demand and of price, and to adjust their actions accordingly" (*Principles of Economics*, p. 783).

[2] Cf. the tables in [Cd. 2337] pp. 87-90.

The Protectionist argument, by which this proof is attempted, turns principally upon certain incidents connected with the modern development of large-scale industrial organisation.   Stated as plausibly as possible, it falls into three divisions, referring respectively to (1) the dumping of surplus produce into England; (2) similar dumping out of England; and (3) the general development of Kartels and Trusts.

§ 11. In the first place, surplus produce is sometimes "dumped" into this country.   In bad times foreign manufacturers do not want to spoil their own market by selling in it cheap.   Neither do they want to disorganise their staff by shutting down their works.   Consequently, when practicable, it is very convenient for them to *dump their surplus* abroad and spoil the market of somebody else.   This policy, when the British market is selected, is, of course, directly advantageous to us, because it enables us to buy what we want at low prices.   But, on the other hand, it has an indirect influence detrimental to the stability of our industry; and nobody can say *a priori* whether the good or the evil result is likely to be the greater. So much can be clearly proved, and ought to be conceded at once by the supporters of Free Trade. When, however, it is argued that this circumstance justifies the establishment of some form of protective tariff, the case is different.

First, a study of the actual facts shows that, in relation to the whole body of our trade, surplus dumping is a trivial incident whose disturbing effects are small.   This point is well illustrated by the recent experience of the iron industry.   In 1902 the German crisis led to a large amount of "dumped"

iron and steel coming to this country. The extracts
from trade journals, which Mr. Schloss prints as an
appendix to his *Memorandum to the Board of Trade*
(in Cd. 1761), do not, however, indicate any great
disturbance in England as a consequence. We are
again and again told that, in spite of the low prices of
the dumped goods, "local steel-makers still adhere
firmly to their quotations." Furthermore, an inspection of the figures concerning employment in the iron
and steel trades, published in the *Labour Gazette*, does
not indicate that 1902 differed appreciably from other
years, either in the number of the men employed or
the number of "shifts" worked per man per week.

If, however, the evil is small, it is the more
necessary to assure ourselves that measures designed
to mitigate it would themselves be free from indirect
ill consequences. But, unfortunately, it does not
appear that any of the protective devices that have
been suggested are at once innocuous and practicable.

One plan that readily presents itself is prohibitive
discriminating duties upon cargoes intended to be
dumped. By this means Customs officials could
apparently checkmate the intending "dumper." But
there is a fundamental difficulty in the way. The
dumper himself is the only person who need know
what his selling price is going to be! In an
imaginary world of "protectionist men" he would
perhaps hand on to the Customs officer all essential
information. In the real world, however, he will
certainly refrain from doing this. If necessary, he
can make consignments at full prices to an agent
at Southampton, instructing him that the goods—
which have not, of course, been dumped into England

from abroad—are forthwith to be dumped from one part of England to another. No scheme has yet been suggested by which evasions of this kind can be prevented. The plan of imposing discriminating duties upon "dumped," as distinguished from other, imports of the same commodity must, therefore, be regarded as outside the range of practical politics.[1]

A second device is Professor Ashley's scheme for empowering the Executive, without resort to Parliament, to impose temporary high duties on all imports of a particular class at such times as surplus dumping seems likely to do more harm than ordinary imports do good.[2] Under an autocracy, incorruptible and omniscient, this plan might, no doubt, succeed. But political proposals have to be considered in the concrete. No responsible statesman supposes that, in the matter of taxation, Parliament will consent to waive its present powers. In such circumstances it is mere academic theorising to suggest that duties can be imposed at one moment and removed at another just as the occasion demands. Professor Ashley's plan may be advisable in some ideal society, but it is scarcely applicable to the actual conditions of the United Kingdom.

A third device is exemplified in the scale of duties provisionally suggested for the iron and steel industry by Mr. Chamberlain's Tariff Commission.[3] This consists in the permanent imposition of duties ranging

---

[1] The Canadian anti-dumping law differs essentially from the policy adumbrated in the text, in that it does not appear to discriminate between different cargoes of the same goods.

[2] *The Tariff Problem*, p. 133.

[3] *Report*, § 88.

up to 10 per cent. But duties of this order would be wholly ineffective against those goods which the commissioners inform us are flooded into our market at slaughter prices. This point is not merely admitted, but strongly emphasised, by Professor Ashley. After giving instances of the kind of reduction at which the surpluses are sometimes sold, he writes: " To meet such prices, duties of 50 or 75 per cent *ad valorem* may be needed, or even prohibition." [1] Nor is this all. The distinguished Professor Dietzel has well shown, in a recent issue of the *Economic Journal*, that low duties would not even *mitigate* the danger of surplus dumping. " A moderate system of Protection," he declares, " affords no security that the floods due to over-production in other countries will not wash away the tariff wall." [2] A country with a surplus tries to spread that surplus over a wide area. Since the normal price in Protectionist tends to exceed that in Free Trade countries by the amount of the duty, it has no inducement to send more to the latter than to the former group. One may even argue—in this diverging from Professor Dietzel—that, if the duty is *ad valorem*, the danger of surplus dumping is actually greater in Protectionist countries, since, whereas, in a Free Trade country, the fall in selling price and in price received is equal, in a Protectionist country, the duty payable being diminished, the price received falls less than the selling price.[3] This point is, no doubt, of little practical interest, since it assumes *ad valorem* duties to be assessed on declared values. The broad conclu-

---

[1] *The Tariff Problem*, p. 133.
[2] *Economic Journal*, March 1905, p. 2.
[3] Cf. my paper, " Professor Dietzel on Dumping," *ib.* Sept. 1905.

sion, that moderate protection is unlikely to diminish the danger of dumping, remains, however, intact.

Hence, it appears that the only remedy, at once effective and practicable, against this evil is the imposition of permanent high duties upon the importation of commodities likely to be dumped. To a proposal of this kind it would suffice to reply by a reference to the evident costliness of the remedy as compared with the triviality of the evil involved. But a more conclusive answer is available. The *permanence* of the duties would almost certainly reverse the steadying influence which, under Professor Ashley's ideal plan of continuous adjustment, their occasional imposition might be expected to produce. The reason for this is evident. While surplus dumping increases fluctuations, ordinary imports diminish them. Their expansion checks upward, and their contraction downward, oscillations of price. Take, for example, the case of a strike in the iron trade. Under our present system rising prices draw German iron to England. Even so, the disorganisation of the secondary industries which use iron as a raw material is considerable. But, if imports were impeded by the presence of a high tariff, their difficulties would be still greater. For every three men who now lose their employment there might then be four or five. In view, therefore, of the fact that the proportion of the imports which are, to those which are not, "dumped" must always be extremely small, a policy of general exclusion as a remedy against surplus dumping bears a perilous resemblance to one of general starvation in mitigation of the dangers of an occasional debauch.

§ 12. In the second place, it may be argued that Protection has a steadying effect, in that, by checking re-imports, it facilitates dumping from the protected country when times are bad. *Pro tanto*, this argument is valid. The provision of an effective means for the disposal of surplus acts upon the industries interested in much the same way as the practice of making for stock. On the other hand, however, when an industry, in times of general depression, steadies itself by dumping surplus abroad, it unsteadies the more advanced industries of its own country. The whole purpose of its action is to maintain the prices of raw materials against them, though these prices are falling in the markets of their foreign rivals. As a consequence, those rivals may be enabled to undersell native firms and to take away part of their custom. This result is independent of the question whether the surplus that is dumped abroad augments the fall of prices there. It is due solely to the circumstance that prices are maintained at home——a circumstance for which the power to dump abroad is in part responsible. Though, therefore, Protection, by strengthening this power, may promote stability in some industries, it is unlikely to promote it to any appreciable extent in the industrial system of the country as a whole.

§ 13. In the third place, attention may be directed to the connection that subsists between protective duties and industrial combination. Circumstances are conceivable under which this latter form of organisation would tend to promote stability.[1] If, therefore, these circumstances are realised, it follows that Protection, so far as it involves combination, itself indirectly promotes stability. On the other hand, however, recent experience shows that there is a tendency

[1] Cf. my paper, *loc. cit.*, pp. 440-441.

among combinations of producing firms to frequent disruption from within. So far as this tendency is realised, combination makes strongly against stability. Furthermore, this particular plea for Protection may, perhaps, like that derived from the economies which large-scale production in the sense of Trust formation promotes, be put aside *ab initio* upon more general grounds. *Timeo Danaos et dona ferentes.* To purchase a little stability at the cost of a Trust, or, still worse, a Kartel system, with its power to mulct the consumer and corrupt the Legislature, is not a bargain that commends itself to those who know the facts.

§ 14. The three incidents of modern industry on which the Protectionist argument about stability depends have thus been reviewed. In every case it has been found that the alleged steadying influence is at the best extremely small. There must now be noticed on the other side a broad and deep force making for disturbance. Protection narrows the market open to purchasers in the protected country, and, the narrower the market, as the history of wheat prices in the nineteenth century shows, the greater is the liability to fluctuation. Booms rise higher, depressions sink lower; the hills and the valleys of industry are alike more marked. " When a period of prosperity occurs in a régime of high Protection "—I quote from Professor Dietzel—

there will be a violent inflation in the favourably situated industries. The consumers are obliged to buy from them—as in former times the customers from the guild masters. The level of prices, profits, wages, rises enormously, to sink in like degree. When a period of prosperity occurs in a Free Trade region there will be a rise of prices, profits, and wages, but not in nearly so great a degree as in the protected regions.   Energy is at once employed throughout the world to work towards the restoration of the disturbed equilibrium between demand and supply, and hence to prevent the waves rising too high. Foreign competition, like oil poured on the sea, moderates the tide of the national industrial system.[1]

In my opinion — the point is not one that is susceptible of rigid proof—this broad general tendency altogether outweighs the special incidents on the other side to which reference has been made.   In spite, therefore, of recent developments in industrial combination, the words addressed by Professor Marshall to the Co-operative Congress in 1885 seem to me still substantially true : " Protection has been proposed as a remedy for the inconstancy of industry ; I believe that all reasonable arguments and all practical experience prove that it much increases that inconstancy." [2] If this conclusion is accepted, it follows from our previous reasoning that Protection is likely to increase, rather than to diminish, both the average number of men out of work and the fluctuations, at once of unemployment and of the unemployed.

§ 15. On all counts, therefore, the thesis that Protection would increase the National Welfare, even though it diminished the National Dividend, has broken down.   Our *prima facie* conclusion that, because it is likely to lessen the amount of that dividend, it is likely also to lessen welfare, becomes therefore a final conclusion.

§ 16. So far the argument has been mainly economic.   In regard, however, to current proposals

---

[1] *Economic Journal*, March 1905, p. 9.
[2] Address to the Co-operative Congress 1885.

for " Tariff Reform," economic considerations, though scientifically interesting, are not of first-rate import- ance.   It is upon practical considerations that the issue raised by these proposals really depends.   In spite, therefore, of the fact that, in referring to matters of general politics the economist is quitting his proper sphere, I cannot avoid some reference to these con- siderations.   To do so would be the more difficult in that, on the practical side, the case against a return to Protection appears to me quite decisive.   I am not thinking merely of the intellectual difficulty of selecting the right cases for that policy and of apply- ing it at the right time.   That is a minor matter. What signifies is that, in England, the supreme financial authority is, not a bureaucracy, but a Ministry sub- ject to the control of Parliament.   In view of the many and great interests which a protective tariff might affect, it is too much to hope that those who controlled it would be left unhampered in the con- templation of their intellectual task.   The need of con- ciliating supporters and of avoiding an adverse division might force them on occasions to modify their proposals —not, perhaps, in the direction most conformable to the intellectual ideal.   It was said of a certain American tariff that the only kind of manufacture to which it essentially related was the manufacture of a President of the United States.   Dangers of that class cannot be ruled out as impossible even in our own country, and the prospect of them has to be reckoned with when the chances are weighed that a really scientific tariff would be framed.   Furthermore, even if it be granted that, in its first form, the tariff would be good for the National Dividend, can we seriously suppose that either the number or the magnitude of the duties embraced under it would remain unaltered? When Protection has been granted to one industry, it is extremely difficult to refuse it to others. When it has been granted at all, it is extremely difficult, in bad times, to reject the plea, which is certain to be made, that the extent of the protection should be augmented. But, if that is difficult, what prospect is there that duties, once imposed, will, when the interests of the State require it, be rigorously reduced or removed? Certain politicians are continually observing that, despite the example offered to them by England, foreign countries steadfastly continue in the paths of Protection, and this, they hold, is an argument against Free Trade. To their opponents, on the other hand, a different and less encouraging inference suggests itself. When duties are imposed, businesses come to be started whose profits depend upon their continuance. Alone, perhaps, no one group of them is strong enough to influence the Legislature. But they are aware of that fact, and, in consequence, combine to resist the introduction of freer trade in one another's commodities. The passage of the recent tariff law through the German Reichstag afforded an excellent object lesson of the working of tariff regulation in practice. In the final result the agrarians contrived to force through Parliament, in the face of Governmental opposition, a set of minimum duties which deliberately sacrifice the general good to the interests of a particular party. The history of the United States teaches the same lesson. During the Civil War high duties were imposed simply for the sake of revenue. After the re-establishment of peace—

G

each year schemes of reduction and reform were brought forward, Commissions were appointed, Bills were elaborated and considered, but the reform was put off from year to year. . . . Gradually, as the organisation of industry in the country adapted itself more closely to the tariff as it was, the feeling that no reform was needed obtained a steady hold. . . . The extreme protective system, which had been at the first a temporary expedient for aiding in the struggle for the Union, adopted hastily and without any thought of deliberation, gradually became accepted as a permanent institution. . . . The result was that the tariff gradually became exclusively and distinctly a protective measure; it included almost all the protective duties put on during the war, added many more to them, and no longer contained the purely revenue duties of the war.[1]

Thus, experience confirms the conclusion to which general considerations point, that "Protection, when once it has taken root, is likely to extend beyond the limits at first assigned to it and is very difficult to extirpate."[2]   Nor is the danger merely economic. "There are also to be apprehended those evils other than material which Protection brings in its train,— the loss of purity in politics, the unfair advantage given to those who wield the powers of jobbery and corruption, and the growth of 'sinister interest.'"[3] This is the practical case—and, in my opinion, it is much stronger than the economic case—against the proposals which have recently been adumbrated by Mr. Chamberlain's Tariff Commission.

[1] Taussig, *Tariff History of the United States*, p. 173.
[2] Professors Edgeworth, Marshall, and others: *Times*, August 15, 1903.
[3] *Ib.* In the original sentence is also included, "the unjust distribution of wealth."

PART II
PREFERENTIAL IMPORT DUTIES

CHAPTER I

§ 1. I DO not propose in this book to discuss preferential arrangements in general. The effects of such arrangements depend on their detailed character. Evidently, England would gain under a scheme securing for her a large preference in colonial markets on condition that she should tax foreign imports of ostrich feathers at the rate of one farthing per ton. As evidently, she would lose under a hypothetical scheme pressed to a like extremity in the opposite direction. The point of current interest is to know how she would fare under the actual scheme that has been adumbrated by Mr. Chamberlain. This is the *Direct Business Question.* I shall discuss it first, not because I consider that the answer to it has a specially important bearing upon the practical issue, but because it is, unlike the political question, one on which economic science is competent to throw some light.

On its business side, then, the essence of Mr. Chamberlain's plan is to purchase certain tariff concessions from the Colonies by a modification in their favour of our existing fiscal system. The chief part of the change contemplated is the substitution for the present arrangement of one under which foreign corn (except maize) is taxed 2s. per quarter, and foreign dairy produce and meat (except bacon) 5 per cent, while, on the other hand, remissions equal in amount to the revenue so raised are granted upon tea, sugar, coffee and cocoa. The problem, from the standpoint of the United Kingdom, is to balance the advantages to be purchased against the price to be paid for them.

§ 2. The credit, or passive, side of the account may be considered first. It is almost certain that, in return for our concessions, the Colonies would grant us some further preference upon certain of the goods that we are accustomed to sell to them. From this it is certain that we should derive *some* advantage. The magnitude of that advantage depends upon the character of the preference granted. Since this is not at present known, any estimate of quantities is necessarily based upon guesswork.

There are, however, certain observations of a critical nature that throw light upon the problem. In the first place, the advantage is certain to be much smaller than is popularly supposed. Mr. Chamberlain, for example, has suggested that it may be measured by the value of the extra exports that we should be enabled to send to colonial markets, and he has added that the wages of the working classes would be enhanced by the whole amount paid to those engaged in making these exports. This opinion is obviously false; for it involves the proposition that, if a manufacturer sells £100 worth of extra goods annually, his income is increased by the whole £100 instead of, as is of course the case, merely by the profits upon that amount of turn-over.

In the second place, though the extent and character of the preference to be accorded to us in return for our concessions is not at present known, we are not wholly in the dark concerning it. The evidence, I think, warrants the following guess. The additional preferences granted to us in consequence of Mr. Chamberlain's scheme, over and above those that would be granted apart from that scheme, would be given, not by reductions of duties upon our goods, but by increases upon those of foreign origin, and the amount of these increases would not, on the average, exceed the 25 per cent of the present rates suggested by the representatives of the Cape and Natal at the last colonial conference. The often-quoted observation of Mr. Fielding to the effect that, as between the British and the Canadian producers, the reductions of duty had already gone far enough, and the fact that the proposed British concessions are widely regarded as a return for tariff favours already received, may be cited as evidence that the above estimate is not unduly pessimistic.

Upon this basis I suggest that the appended rough method of estimating our gain would be accepted as reasonable by a majority of economists. According to the Fiscal Blue-book,[1] the average *ad valorem* equivalent of the import duties levied upon the principal articles of British export by the self-governing Colonies are as follows :

Canada	16%
Australian Commonwealth . .	6%
New Zealand	9%
South African Customs Union . .	6%

---

[1] [Cd. 1761] p. 172.

In 1901 the values of the exports of British and Irish produce to the different Colonies were, roughly :

Canada	£7,000,000
Australian Commonwealth .	21,000,000
New Zealand. . . .	5,000,000
South Africa	17,000,000

Weighting the rates of duty imposed in the different Colonies according to the amount of our exports sent to each of them respectively, we get a general average level of duty of something between 7 and 8 per cent. Our position, therefore, is somewhat as it would be if colonial duties upon our goods were uniform at 8 per cent.

It is upon this that we are to be benefited, as against the foreigner, by an increase in his payment to the tune of 25 per cent. That is to say, the duties against us are to be maintained at 8 per cent, and those against foreigners raised to 10 per cent.

In order to calculate the monetary value of this preference, we need to form some judgment as to its probable effect, on the one hand, upon the amount, and, on the other, upon the price of our exports to the Colonies. Our gain would be represented approximately by the change in price multiplied by the aggregate of our sales in colonial markets under the new system. The *maximum* possible rise of price is, clearly, equal to the rate of the extra tax, namely, 2 per cent. Our exports to the self-governing Colonies may be reckoned at some £50,000,000 annually, while the *maximum* of foreign imports into the Colonies, which we might conceivably displace, is estimated by the Board of Trade at £26,000,000. Consequently, the limit of possible gain is 2 per cent of £76,000,000, or about a million and a half. It is, however, exceedingly improbable, either that the price would rise to the full extent of the extra tax, or that, in response to a 2 per cent preference, we should displace foreign competition in the Colonies by anything approaching £26,000,000 worth of goods. Furthermore, the more we succeed in displacing the foreigner, the smaller is the rise of price likely to be, so that a very great increase of price and a very great increment of trade are not likely to go together. Nor is this all. In so far as we ousted foreign merchandise from colonial markets, we should divert it in part to neutral markets, with the result that the demand of these for British goods would fall. Even if the capital and labour in competing countries, which was diverted from making exports for Canada and Australia, restricted itself henceforward to the home trade, there might be a corresponding slackening in the demand for British goods—this time in the competing countries themselves. When all these things are taken into account, —the probable failure of colonial prices to rise by nearly the full rate of the duty, the imperfect manner in which we are likely to displace foreign competitors in the colonial market, and the probability of our finding ourselves confronted with more stringent competition elsewhere—it is not, I think, to be expected that the net gain would much exceed half a million a year.

It may, indeed, be urged that, as the Colonies expand, the amount of this benefit will grow. Since, however, colonial expansion is sure to be accompanied by the development of industries manufacturing goods now supplied by us, the growth is not likely to be large. It will be of little avail that our manufacturers are favoured as against foreign rivals, if, through the duties still retained against them, they are beaten by the Colonists themselves. Of course, were the spirit engendered by the new policy to lead ultimately to Free Trade within the Empire, the result might be different. The suggestion, however, that the return of the Mother Country to Protection would prove a first step towards the Colonies' abandonment of it is not one in whose support any evidence is forthcoming. It appears, therefore, improbable that, even in the long-run, the value of the colonial concessions to our trade would be other than small.

§ 3. I turn to the debit, or active, side of the balance, the cost involved in the proposed alteration of our own tariff system. The most obvious item under this head, and the one which first demands attention, is the direct payment we should be required to make to colonial agriculturalists. The amount of this payment depends upon the extent to which the price of their produce in our markets would rise. To determine it, therefore, we need to investigate that problem.

At this point, however, it is advisable to interpose certain critical observations. In the first place, the issue is frequently prejudiced by two erroneous pieces of statistical reasoning. Of these the one belongs to Mr. Chamberlain's supporters, and consists in tables drawn up to show that prices, after the imposition of a tax, have, in some cases, been no higher than prices before the tax. Such reasoning proves nothing with regard to the effect of the tax, because it is impossible to eliminate the other causes which have contributed to the statistical result. The question at issue is, not how much higher the price will be *after* the tax than it was *before*, but how much higher it will be than it would have been if the tax had not been there.

The other bad statistical argument belongs to Mr. Chamberlain's opponents. It consists in a comparison of prices in England with those in other countries where there are import duties. Concerning this argument the correct conclusion is, I think, as follows: When there are two countries, each of which imports a considerable quantity of the taxed commodity, and, when the one has been free-trading, and the other has established a given duty, for a considerable time, the difference between the price in the two countries may be expected to exceed what it would have been had both been free-trading, by the full amount of the tax. The actual difference need not be equal to the tax, even on the average, because the conditions of the two countries need not be such that, save for the tax, the price of the particular commodity would have been the same in the one as in the other. It may, however, be safely affirmed that, when the commodities, whose prices are taken, are really identical, the tax in the one country will tend to raise the price there relatively to the price in the other country by its whole amount.

This result has, however, been treated by Mr. Asquith, Sir William Harcourt, and, perhaps also, Lord Goschen, as equivalent to the conclusion that the duty makes the price in the taxing country higher by the whole tax *than it would otherwise have been.* Such reasoning is fallacious because it ignores the possible effect of a German tax upon the price of the taxed commodity outside of Germany, But, in certain cases, the tax will so operate upon demand as to lower the price in the world-market, and this to such a degree that the German price might conceivably exceed the English price by the whole tax, and yet be practically identical with what it would have been if the tax had never been imposed.

In addition to the above, there are two bad economic arguments which it is also necessary to dismiss. Both of these are the property of Mr. Chamberlain's supporters. The first refers in particular to the case of wheat, and is to the effect that, even though the price of that commodity rise under a tax, the rise will be balanced by an equivalent fall in the price of various by-products, such as bran and offals. The answer, of course, is that the British farmer will not increase his production, unless the rate of re-muneration, which he expects for the whole of it taken together, is increased. If he is to lose on the by-products as much as he gains on the staples he will not be induced by the duty to grow more than he does at present. The fall in bran and offals, which is expected to result from the increased home production of wheat, would, no doubt, afford some set-off to the rise in the price of that commodity ; but this set-off would only be partial. The broad effect of the duties must, therefore, be to render agricultural produce in general more expensive.

In rejoinder to the above the second bad economic argument in Mr. Chamberlain's armoury is usually invoked. Under purely protective duties, it is admitted, prices might rise; but, under preferential duties which leave colonial imports free, they certainly would not. I do not pause to ask the old question how, in that case, the new policy could be expected to fulfil its advocates' many promises of benefit to the British farmer; for that question has been asked often, and has never yet been answered. It is more profitable to face the problem directly. The solution appears to be that the result which Mr. Chamberlain's supporters proclaim to be *certain* is *possible* in abstract theory. Conditions are conceivable in which the duties he contemplates would so stimulate the development of railways and other transport facilities in our Colonies that, in the long-run, the price of their products would reach a level as low as, or even lower than, that which they would have attained in the ordinary course of things. But this result, though conceivable, is, even in the abstract, highly improbable. It implies that the conditions of agricultural production here and in the Colonies are at present fixed in a region of unstable equilibrium, and that, without preferential duties, the small impetus required to start them moving from thence will not be given. In the concrete the answer is still more conclusive. There is ample evidence that the desired movement has already begun. The Canadian North-West does not need the touch of a preferential fairy prince to waken her, but is already alive with youthful energy. Hence, it is practically certain that the preferential character of the proposed taxes would not prevent them from raising prices above the level which would otherwise have been reached.

§ 4. I turn, therefore, to consider directly the extent to which prices are likely to rise. In the abstract, a formula can be obtained which states the amount of the change quite definitely in terms of certain variables. The factors upon which it depends are, in technical language, the elasticities of demand and supply and the quantities produced in the different countries concerned. We can say absolutely that, under conditions of diminishing returns, the price will rise more nearly to the full extent of the tax, (1) the more urgent is the British demand for the taxed commodity, or, in other words, the more " necessary " that commodity is to us; (2) the smaller is the increase in the quantity of the commodity offered in our market from home and colonial sources in consequence of a given price change; (3) the greater is the decrease in the quantity offered from the taxed source; (4) the greater is the quantity supplied from the taxed relatively to that from the untaxed source.[1] To

---

[1] This conclusion can be expressed analytically as follows :—Let A, B, C be the present supplies to the British market from foreign, colonial, and home sources respectively, e_1, e_2, e_3 their elasticities, and η (a negative quantity) the elasticity of the British demand curve. Let that part of the colonial supply, which is at present sent to foreign markets and could be readily diverted to ours, be neglected as unimportant, and let it be assumed that means are found to prevent evasion by false certificates of origin and so on. Then, if T be the tax, and $\Delta\pi$ the consequent rise in price, and if we assume that throughout the small portions of the demand and supply curves, with which we are concerned, the elasticities are constant, we obtain as a first approximation :

$$\Delta\pi = T\frac{e_1 A}{e_1 A + e_2 B + e_3 C - \eta(A + B + C)}.$$

The same result, in another and, for some purposes, more convenient, notation, may be written thus : Let A, B, C represent the present foreign, colonial, and British *production*, e_1, e_2, e_3 the

translate these results into actual figures, it is, however, necessary to know the *facts* about elasticity; and, unfortunately, no reliable information on that subject exists. Consequently, we can only apply our formula by guessing the value of some of the variables involved in it; and, concerning the right guesses to make, it is inevitable that wide differences of opinion should exist.

The problem is undoubtedly easiest, and the element of uncertainty least, in the case of the suggested duty upon wheat. A trifling rise in the price of a prime necessary of life is not likely to check the consumption of it to any appreciable extent. Consequently, the price can only be prevented from rising to the full extent of the tax by the substitution of colonial and home-grown wheat for a part of the supplies which we at present draw from abroad. Now, the total wheat crop of foreign countries amounts to some 284 million quarters annually, and that of the Colonies and India to some 45 million quarters. Consequently, unless the "' elasticity " of supply from colonial sources is greater than that from foreign sources, a change of price capable of adding one million quarters to the colonial growth might be expected to add some six million to

respective elasticities of *production*, and η_1, η_2, η_3 those of demand in the three sources respectively. Then

$$\Delta \pi = T \frac{e_1 A - \eta_1 A}{e_1 A + e_2 B + e_3 C - (\eta_1 A + \eta_2 B + \eta_3 C)}.$$

Since the British price embraces cost of carriage, we should expect that, *ceteris paribus*, the colonial and foreign elasticities in respect of British price changes would be greater than the British elasticities.

I have had the great advantage of reading an unpublished note upon this part of the subject by Mr. C. P. Sanger, of University College, London, though he is not, of course, responsible for any of the opinions here expressed.

the foreign growth. Therefore, if we are to obtain from the world at large the same amount of wheat after our preference as before it, we must expect the price of colonial wheat to rise about six times as much as the price of foreign wheat falls. That is to say, we must expect the price in England to rise by about six-sevenths of the amount of the tax. We have, however, to take account of the fact that part of the deficiency in our foreign imports would be made up, not from colonial, but from home sources. Our present output of some seven million quarters is not, as a matter of fact, likely to expand much in consequence of a small price change, but, if we assume an expansion proportionately equal to that of colonial crops, we get a corrected rise of price equal to about five-sixths of the amount of the tax. I, therefore, suggest that the rise of price due to the tax be put at 1s. 8d. per quarter.

This is, I think, a result which may be regarded with a fair amount of confidence. The probability is considerable that the rise in price would not be less than 1s. 8d. a quarter, and strong arguments can be urged for the view that it would be more.[1] With regard, however, to the other items of Mr. Chamberlain's programme, I am at a loss to see how anything of value can be said except that the rise of price will be proportionately a good deal less than it is in the case of wheat. The demand for these other commodities is probably fairly elastic in all countries, but

[1] For the above argument assumes that the foreign demand, as well as the English demand, is perfectly inelastic. The presence of rye substitutes may, however, render this assumption invalid, and would, therefore, cause the price to rise further than I have indicated.

we cannot say how elastic; they are capable of being substituted for one another, and also for commodities which are not taxed, but we cannot say to what extent; there is, presumably, a certain area which may be regarded as a common market for them, but it is not a world-market, such as there is for wheat, and we cannot say how far in any direction it is likely to stretch; and, finally, for meat and dairy produce, the statistics of consumption and production are hopelessly defective. For all these reasons, it seems to me inevitable that any guess as to the effect of import duties upon prices must be liable to enormous error. Nevertheless, for my purpose, it is essential that such a guess should be made. I have done my best to form a judgment from the material available, and my guess, for what it is worth, is that, on the average, the price of barley and oats may be expected to rise by not less than a quarter, and that of the other commodities by not less than a half of the tax.

If this solution of the price problem be accepted, the extra payment made by British consumers to colonial agriculturists works out as below, provided that the colonial imports continue at their present rate:

On Wheat and Flour, 5·8 million qrs., at 1s. 8d.
    per qr. £482,000
On Butchers' Meat (excepting pig-meat), £6·4 million,
    at $\frac{1}{2}$ of 5% 160,000
On Dairy Produce, £7·4 million, at $\frac{1}{2}$ of 5% . . 185,000

                        Total . . £827,000

It will be noticed that the foregoing calculation assumes that the colonial imports remain unchanged. Such an assumption is illegitimate, because it is only through the substitution of colonial for foreign supplies that prices in England are prevented from rising much further than I have estimated. Furthermore, the reason why I have put the rise in the price of fodder grains so low is that maize will probably be substituted for them to a large extent, and bacon, the finished product of maize, to a small extent. Hence we should expect the price of maize to change similarly with the price of barley, and, as our imports of it amount to some twelve million £ worth, this would involve an additional payment from England to the maize-growers of over a quarter of a million. If this be so, the aggregate direct payment we should have to make to the Colonies—the American maize-growers being, from this point of view, counted along with them—would amount to something like £1,000,000 a year.

§ 5. There are, however, other items to be considered. We may, indeed, suppose, in accordance with previous reasoning,[1] that, as regards the general ratio of interchange, between British and foreign goods, the proposed tariff system would operate in much the same way as the present one. It has, however, still to be decided under which of the two (1) the loss of consumers' surplus on the consumption that is destroyed, and (2) the proportion of their revenue that the inhabitants of the country escape from paying, is likely to be the greater.

The latter element is the easier to discuss. Our foreign imports of wheat are about 19 million quarters, of barley and oats about 10 million quarters, of butchers' meat about $18\frac{1}{2}$ million £ worth, of dairy produce about 34 million £ worth. If, therefore, our importation were not altered by the proposed scheme of

[1] Cf. Part I. Chap. I. § 10.

taxation, and if prices were to change in the manner suggested above, the revenue collected and the payment escaped by the country would work out as follows:

	Revenue. £ million	Payment escaped by the Country. £ million
On 19 million qrs. wheat at 2s. per qr.	1·9	$(1 \cdot 9 \times \frac{1}{6} =)$ ·32
On 10 million qrs. barley and oats at 2s. per qr.	1·0	$(1 \times \frac{3}{4} =)$ ·75
On 18½ million £ worth of butchers' meat at 5%	·9	$(\cdot 9 \times \frac{1}{2} =)$ ·45
On 34 million £ worth of dairy produce at 5%	1·7	$(1 \cdot 7 \times \frac{1}{2} =)$ ·85
	£5·5	£2·37

On this showing, the gain accruing to the country would amount to between two and two-and-a-half million pounds. It is, however, evident that the hypothesis of *unchanged foreign imports*, upon which the preceding table depends, is not compatible with the changes of price that have been supposed. In order to these small price changes in England, it is essential that the diminution in the quantity of the foreign imports should be considerable. In the case of fodder grains in particular it is to be expected, as has already been observed, that barley and oats would, in a great measure, yield place to maize. On the whole, therefore, in our final estimate there must appear considerably smaller items both under the head of revenue received and under that of burden escaped. How great a reduction ought to be made it is impossible to guess except in the roughest manner. It is, however, very improbable that the burden escaped would in the end exceed a million or a million and a half.

Furthermore, over against this, there has to be set

a similar saving already made upon the revenue from tea, sugar, etc., since it is very improbable that the price of these commodities is now increased by the full amount of our taxation. If, therefore, we abandoned a revenue from tea and sugar equal to that received from the new tariff, the net gain from the change would be less than the burden escaped under that tariff. It would be equal to this burden minus the burden escaped under the present tariff. What this sum would amount to we cannot do more than guess. I should imagine, however, that the net gain would be well under £1,000,000.

§ 6. There remains the loss of consumers' surplus on the part of the consumption which the tax destroys. It is scarcely possible to say whether this would be larger under the present or under the proposed system ; for, while the demand for wheat is probably less elastic than that for tea and sugar, the demand for dairy produce, butchers' meat, and fodder grain is probably more so. Perhaps the proposed change would yield some small advantage under this head.

If, then, we finally reckon up the active side of our account, there appears an item of something over a million to be paid to the Colonies, an item of something under a million of burden escaped, and another small advantage in respect of the loss of consumers' surplus. On the whole, therefore, it seems that, so far, the proposed system would work out in very much the same way as the present one. Hence, when we compare this side of the account with the credit or passive side, a favourable balance emerges of some half million pounds a year due to the concessions purchased from the Colonies.

§ 7. But an essential point has been omitted. Against this *probable* addition to the amount of our national wealth, there has to be set a *certain* injury to its distribution. Under this head two points have to be considered :

First, a shilling exacted from the consumers of wheat means, on the average, more real suffering than an equal sum from the consumers of tea and sugar ; for the proportion of our annual wheat supply consumed by the very poor is probably larger than the proportion of our annual tea and sugar supply ; and wheat is the commodity whose price under the new system would be affected most seriously. Consequently, though the wealth of the country were greater under the proposed than under the existing plan, its welfare might be smaller. This consideration is important.

The second point is still more so. Under the preferential scheme, a considerable part of the burden escaped by the country is not escaped by the consumers. Rather, a large payment is exacted from them, and paid to the home agricultural interest. Our present home production probably stands somewhat as follows :

Wheat . . .	6·7 million quarters.
Barley and Oats . .	28·6 „
Butchers' Meat [1] . .	£42,000,000
Dairy Produce [2] . .	£40,000,000

Multiplying the estimated change of prices by the

[1] Estimated by a combination of the assumption that 1000 cattle mean 67½, and 1000 sheep 21½ tons of meat annually, with the average of Sauerbeck's wholesale price statistics during the decade ending 1902.

[2] A guess : probably an underestimate.

present home production, we get the extra payment ultimately made by consumers to landlords as under:

Wheat: 1s. 8d. per qr., on 6·7 million qrs .	£558,000
Barley and Oats: 6d. per qr. on 28·6 million qrs.	715,000
Butchers' Meat: 2½ per cent on £42,000,000	1,050,000
Dairy Produce: „ . „ 40,000,000	1,000,000
Approximate total . .	£3,300,000

Now, if the average wealth of that part of the agricultural interest to which this transfer of wealth is made were about equal to that of the average consumer, the change would, from a national standpoint, be a matter of small importance. But, the condition supposed is not in fact realised. No doubt, it is often suggested that the part of the agricultural interest that would be benefited by the proposed policy is the relatively poor class of tenant farmers and agricultural labourers. In Mr. Chamberlain's Welbeck speech, for instance, the benefits anticipated for these persons were expounded in glowing terms, while the very existence of another important class—the owners of agricultural land—was ignored altogether. Economists, however, are aware that, if duties were imposed upon agricultural imports, it would be to this class that nearly the whole advantage thereby conferred upon agriculture would, in the long-run, accrue.

This proposition can be established fairly satisfactorily by general reasoning. Though, no doubt, tenants with long leases would retain part of the gain for a time, it is evident that, when leases come to be renewed, the landlord has the whip hand, and can raise rents to match the improved prices of agricultural produce. Nor is it in the least relevant to reply that rents are largely influenced by private friendliness and other non-economic considerations. For these influences are operating already just as effectively as they are likely to do under Mr. Chamberlain's proposals. Non-economic and economic factors both play their part. But, when the former remain constant and the latter change, the fact that the former are in existence affords no ground for doubting that the new cause which has been introduced will be followed by its appropriate effect. This general argument is confirmed *a posteriori* by statistical evidence. As everybody knows, it is the landlords whom the recent prolonged fall of prices has struck most severely. Their rents have moved in about the same proportion as agricultural prices. Indeed, the parallel between the changes which have occurred in these prices and in incomes assessed to ownership of "lands" during the last forty years has been very striking. In the following table the price movements as between successive decades are compared with the movements in the value of lands as between the final years of each decade.

TABLE [1]

Value of Lands in the U. K.	Unweighted Index Number of Wheat, Barley, Oats, Prime and Middling Beef and Mutton, Pork and Bacon.
Between	Between
1860 and 1870 rose 10 per cent.	1850-9 and 1870-9 rose 10·5 p.c.
1870 ,, 1880 ,, 8 ,,	1860-9 ,, 1870-9 ,, 11·5 ,,
1880 ,, 1890 fell 16 ,,	1870-9 ,, 1880-9 fell 14·8 ,,
1890 ,, 1900 ,, 9 ,,	1880-9 ,, 1890-9 ,, 15·5 ,,

[1] In this table the figures for Irish lands for 1860 have been estimated from the values of 1862, the earliest year in which they are recorded. The smallness of the fall in lands between 1890 and 1900 as compared with the fall in price is partly explained by the passing of the Agricultural Rating Act.

It may, indeed, be answered that, even granted that the recent fall in prices has hit the landlords hardest, it does not follow that its effects have been confined to them. It is still possible that these effects have also been largely felt by the agricultural labourer. As between the three years beginning with 1880 and the three beginning with 1900 his wages have only risen 9·7 per cent, while wages in general, apart from agriculture, have risen 18·8 per cent.[1] Under these circumstances may we not suppose that the connection between his fortune and the landlord's, which has been maintained through the depression, would continue if an agricultural tariff were to convert bad times to good ?

The answer to this rejoinder is fourfold. In the first place, it must be remembered that, though agricultural wages have not increased so fast as industrial wages, they have, nevertheless, increased considerably. In the second place, their lagging is smaller in reality than in appearance. As Professor Marshall has observed, "the spread of modern notions to agricultural districts causes many of the ablest children born there to leave the fields for the railway or the workshop, to become policemen, or to act as carters or porters in towns,"[2] with the result that those who are left behind in the fields have probably a less share of natural abilities relatively to town dwellers than they had until comparatively recent times. This circumstance would naturally involve a relative decline in their wages. In the third place, an important factor in checking the demand for labourers' services has been

---

[1] Calculated from tables in Cd. 1761, p. 260.
[2] *Principles of Economics*, p. 771 n.

one quite independent of foreign trade, the substitution, namely, of mechanical for muscular power in various mechanical operations.[1]   Lastly—and this reply is of itself sufficient—such part of the retardation in the wage movement as is really connected with cheap imports is traceable to the *continuous fall*, and not to the *absolute lowness*, of agricultural prices.   If these had been merely low, things would have adjusted themselves.   In accordance with well-known economic laws there would have occurred a transference of labour from agriculture to other occupations, until equilibrium between their respective wage-levels was restored.   Since, however, prices were not merely low but falling, supply, though steadily following, failed to come up with demand.   Agricultural labour proving, like all labour, unable to adjust itself quickly to changed conditions, remained, until the last year or two, in excess of the farmer's requirements.   It suffered on account of changes to which it delayed to respond.

The bearing of this analysis upon our immediate problem is decisive.   A fixed duty upon foreign agricultural imports can affect the absolute level of agricultural prices, but, except in the short period of readjustment immediately following its imposition, cannot affect their changes.   These could be influenced only by some kind of "climbing" duty, which Mr. Chamberlain has never ventured to propose.   His fixed duties, therefore, cannot confer any permanent benefit upon the agricultural labourer.   Precisely similar reasoning applies to the farmer.   Hence it follows that the only real beneficiaries of his policy

---

[1] Cf. Marshall, *Principles of Economics*, p. 354.

would be the agricultural landlords. It is they who would pocket the extra payment which our consumers would have to make to the home agricultural interest.

Now, under an economy of peasant proprietors such as prevails in France, it is quite possible that the average wealth of agricultural landlords is less than that of people in general. In Great Britain, however, the average agricultural landlord is certainly much wealthier than the average citizen. Consequently, to put money into his pocket at the expense of the community is to mulct the relatively poor for the endowment of the relatively rich.

It is sometimes, indeed, urged, in reply to this argument, that an increase in the prosperity of landlords reacts upon that of other classes. This answer, however, has no weight. Since the extra wealth secured to the landlords is taken *from* the public, the indirect reflex benefit *to* the public is scarcely likely to compensate for that expense. If any one asserts that it will, he may be invited to revise a number of opinions which usually meet with acceptance. It will follow, for example, that he has only to give his income away in order to obtain a greater income from the reflex benefits showered upon him by those who receive it. I conclude, therefore, that the proposed policy is certain to act injuriously upon the distribution of wealth.

§ 8. Whether this evil would outweigh the good of the probable small increase in the *amount* of wealth cannot be strictly determined. For myself, I am inclined to think that it would do this. But I am content with a less rigorous conclusion. When the whole situation is taken into account, it is improbable that the economic position of the country would be appreciably affected either for good or for evil by the establishment of Mr. Chamberlain's scheme of preferential arrangements with the Colonies.

CHAPTER II

THE GENERAL QUESTION

§ 1. From what has been said it is evident that the issue between the advocates and the opponents of Preferential Arrangements is but little clarified by a purely economic investigation. Its decision must depend upon wider and less precise considerations. The practically important arguments are (1) those which touch the probable effect of the change on the political and moral relations of the different parts of the British Empire; and (2) those which relate to the probable *accompaniments* of the preferential duties now proposed, and the probable future development of the fiscal policy that they would inaugurate in our own country. It is on account of this class of argument that I am myself opposed to the imposition of these duties.

§ 2. I shall begin by examining the probable accompaniments of the proposed change, and must remark, at the outset, that there is a *possible* accompaniment that would considerably strengthen the case for that change. If the new system were introduced in conjunction with a readjustment of the rest of our taxation carefully designed for that purpose, the bad effects upon distribution, that were noted in the last chapter, could be entirely counteracted. There is, however, no indication that any plan of this kind will be adopted. Rather, the accompaniments of Preference, which appear to be *probable*, are twofold.

First, since that policy would involve the imposition of a positive and obvious detriment upon foreign traders, both in this country and in the Colonies, there is a not inconsiderable chance that it would provoke reprisals. It is not a question of whether or not Germany and other countries would be morally justified in resorting to measures of retaliation, but whether, as a matter of fact, they would be likely to do this. Now, even before Mr. Chamberlain's policy was announced, Baron von Richthofen hinted to the British Ambassador that, if "large portions of the British Empire were to give preferential treatment to Great Britain, it would be very difficult to obtain the consent of the Reichstag to the prolongation of most - favoured - nation treatment to Great Britain herself." This suggestion may have been, and, indeed, at the time when it was made, probably was, little more than a piece of diplomatic bluff. But it points to a danger which is real, and which might become very serious if, by treaty arrangements, the Colonies were to grant us Preference through increased duties upon foreigners, and if the Mother Country were to reciprocate the policy of her daughter States. It is probable that we should become involved in numerous tariff discussions, and possible that some of these would lead to tariff wars. Such things are expensive. When, moreover, it is remembered that British exports to foreign countries are about three times as great as those to the self-governing Colonies, it becomes obvious that to risk a foreign attack for the sake of a colonial favour is, however patriotic and imperial, not satisfactory *business*.

Secondly, in view of the present state of public opinion, it appears practically certain that the policy of Preference would not be adopted by Parliament except in company with Protection against imported manufactures, as understood by the Tariff Commission. This accompaniment we have already seen reason to condemn.

Furthermore, as was argued in the same place, a tariff of that kind is almost certain, under the pressure of interested parties, to become more strongly protective as time proceeds, and to carry with it political and moral evils.[1] Hence, even though the preferential duties themselves remained unaltered, the general policy of which they were a part might be expected to grow continually more injurious. The probable accompaniments of Preference in our own country are, therefore, highly undesirable.

§ 3. It may still be answered that the advantages to be secured for the Empire as a political and moral organism are great enough to warrant us in accepting these evils as a necessary means towards them.

To this there are two replies: First, even if it could be proved that Preference would on the whole effect more good than harm, the case for its adoption is not made out. It may be established beyond dispute that, by burning the house over our head, we can win from reluctant nature the succulent glories of roast pork; but, it does not follow that a policy of intermittent incendiarism is one which a wise

---

[1] Cf. Part I. Chap. II. § 16.

man would pursue. Before deciding upon such a
course he would need to inquire, not only whether the
game were worth the candle, but also and primarily
whether there were no better means by which the
same result could be achieved. In the present
instance an alternative to Preference has more than
once been suggested, in the shape of direct or indirect
bounties. Sir James Blyth favours grants from the
Imperial Exchequer for developing agricultural
education, and Professor Davidson for organising
transport facilities in the Colonies. A scheme more
analogous to Mr. Chamberlain's would consist in direct
payments upon imports of colonial produce, calculated
to yield the same advantage to Canada, Australia, New
Zealand, and South Africa, as would be secured to
them under the preferential duties.

Against this scheme the objection is sometimes
urged that it would inflict an injury upon British
agricultural landlords. Whatever reduction it caused
in price would indirectly diminish rents, and thus lead
to a transference of wealth from owners of land to the
community in general. In view, however, of the smallness of our colonial imports, a given payment to the
Colonies through bounties must lower English prices
far less than an equal payment through preferential
duties would raise them. Consequently, the transference of wealth from landlords to consumers under a
scheme of bounties would be considerably less than
the transference *to* them *from* consumers under a preferential policy. While, therefore, a change of distribution must be caused in either case, it would require
a very ardent advocate of vested interests to deny that,
from the point of view of the country as a whole, the

change due to bounties would be considerably the less disadvantageous of the two.

A second objection, frequently urged, is that the burden of a bounty would be an increasing, while that of Preference would be a diminishing one, the reason given being that the proportion of our food supplies drawn from the Colonies may be expected, in the natural course of evolution, greatly to increase. It has latterly become the custom to take this prophecy for granted without any investigation of the facts. A study of Sir William Crookes's *Wheat Problem* [1] is, however, calculated to make one sceptical of the glowing accounts so often given of Canadian possibilities, while, on the other hand, the undeveloped resources of new countries outside the British dominions seem to be deserving of more attention than is generally bestowed upon them. Only three years ago the Professor of Agriculture in Edinburgh University wrote [2] to advocate Protection, upon the ground that the competition of Argentina was likely soon to become greater than the British farmer could bear. It, thus, appears doubtful whether the proportion of our supplies drawn from within the Empire really will be augmented in the natural course, and whether, therefore, even the first step in the above argument can be sustained. This point may, however, be waived ; for, in any case, it is very improbable that the burden of a bounty would grow to any greater extent than that of a preferential duty. The prevalence of the contrary opinion seems to be due to a habit of regarding the whole of any tax as a national sacrifice

---

[1] *E.g.* p. 24.
[2] *Times*, December 15, 1903.

instead of as, in part, a transference of wealth from the people at large to their representatives in the Government. When a more accurate view is taken, it becomes apparent that the burden to be considered ought to be calculated in a different manner. Under a bounty it is equal to the amount of our colonial imports multiplied by the difference between the rate of bounty and the fall of price which it causes; under Preference to these imports multiplied by the rise of price resulting from the tax; the foreigner's "contribution" being subtracted in both cases. In the appended footnote [1] a technical argument is advanced to show that an increase in the proportion of our imports from the Colonies is likely to diminish, and not to increase,

[1] Let A be the supply to the English market from foreign countries: B from the Colonies.

Let e_1, e_2 be the elasticities of the two supplies respectively, η that of the English demand in respect of external sources.

Let T_1 be the tax under the preferential plan; T_2 the bounty under the other plan: Δp_1 the rise of price corresponding to the former, and Δp_2 the fall corresponding to the latter. Let the ratio of the tax to the prevailing price be small.

Then, as a first approximation, the excess of the burden under a bounty over that under Preference $= \{BT_2 - (A+B)\Delta p_2\} - \{(A+B)\Delta p_1 - AT_1\}$.

In order to the Colonies receiving the same endowment under the two plans, $\Delta p_1 B = (T_2 - \Delta p_2)B$.

But $\Delta p_1 = \dfrac{e_1 A}{c_1 A + e_2 B - \eta(A+B)} T_1$, and $\Delta p_2 = \dfrac{e_2 B}{e_1 A + e_2 B - \eta(A+B)} T_2$.

$$\therefore\ T_2 = \frac{e_1 A}{e_1 A - \eta(A+B)} T_1.$$

Hence, the excess of the burden under a bounty over that under Preference is found to be

$$= AT_1 \frac{-\eta(A+B)}{e_1 A - \eta(A+B)}.$$

Since e_1 is positive and η negative, it is clear that, if $(A+B)$ remains constant, every increase in the ratio of B to A involves a decrease in the value of this expression.

I

the excess of the former over the latter of these two quantities.

The real objection to bounties, therefore, is simply that the absolute amount of the burden incurred under them would, in accordance with the reasoning of the preceding footnote, be somewhat greater than that incurred under Preference. This incident, however, is outweighed by the fact that, since a policy of Imperial bounties has not as yet been mixed up with an agitation in behalf of general protection, it could be much more readily introduced without that perilous accompaniment. Such a policy, in fact, would seem to afford a more secure means than preferential duties, to the same Imperial purpose.

§ 4. But this is not all. Behind it there remains a broader question. In advocacy of preferential arrangements it has been eloquently said: "*Let us unite the Empire, the great aspiration of the wisest and the best of your statesmen.*"[1] The broader question is: Would the proposed policy subserve this end, not merely more satisfactorily than bounties, but at all? That question is in no way connected with economics, but I cannot conclude without a brief reference to it.

The claim formally made in behalf of a preferential system is that its adoption would help forward *political* unity. To prove this, its author has appealed to history, and has declared that "commercial union in all previous cases has always preceded closer political federation."[2] This statement is not, however, in accordance with the facts. That famous advocate

---

[1] Mr. Chamberlain at Welbeck, *Times*, Aug. 4, 1904.
[2] Mr. Chamberlain's Address to the Agents-General, Nov. 18, 1903

of Nationalism, Friedrich List, makes a precisely
opposite assertion. "All examples," he writes, "which
history can show are those in which the political
union has led the way and the commercial union has
followed. Not a single instance can be adduced in
which the latter has taken the lead and the former
has grown up from it."[1]   Mr. Chamberlain's one illus-
tration is the German Zollverein. There, indeed, the
seed of commercial union bore political fruit. It
needs, however, but little argument to prove that
between that case and the present there is no analogy.
It is not merely that Germany consists of contiguous
States and the British Empire of ocean-sundered
colonies. The essential point is that the nature of
the commercial union whose results Mr. Chamberlain
applauds was disparate in every respect from that
which he seeks to justify by its example. The policy
which succeeded was the abolition of all duties between
the separate States. The policy which is proposed is
the imposition by the separate States of new duties
upon foreign imports. No inference from the one to
the other can possess the slightest cogency.

But perhaps the main thought of the advocates of
Preference is the less tangible, though not less valuable,
ideal of *moral and sympathetic* unity. If this be
their goal, it must be answered that no reasons
have hitherto been advanced for believing that that
great good would issue from their policy. As the
history of the South African war has shown, colonial
loyalty is not a matter of loaves and fishes. "They
poured out their blood ; they gave us of their treasure ;
they showed that we are one kin, one people, and one

---

[1] *The National System of Political Economy*, p. 126.

nation." [1] All this was done, but it was done "not for the gain of the gold, the getting, the hoarding, the having." Nor is it merely that the moral unity of the Empire can *dispense* with a preferential tonic. There is ground for fear that, like the potion Lucilia proffered to her lord, the supposed love-philtre may prove an irritant poison. It is not a light thing to introduce fresh occasions of friction into the complicated machinery of a world - empire. Discussions about money have been known to sever friends. They may also sever States. The example of the Austro-Hungarian Ausgleich—one far more pertinent than that of the Zollverein—is not encouraging. The late Dr. Petritsch, an Austrian economist of distinction, has drawn the moral in concise terms :

> The economical aspect of the commercial relations between Austria and Hungary present a pretty close analogy to those between the United Kingdom and her Colonies, and one might surmise that identical causes are likely to have identical consequences. It must be observed, too, that Mr. Chamberlain's preferential scheme would entail an entangled network of treaties far more complicated than the negotiations of the Austro-Hungarian Zoll- und Handelsbundniss. There does not seem to exist the faintest ground for believing that the difficulties in conciliating so manifold divergent interests will be less. [2]

Nor can it be rightly answered : " Let us at least try the experiment and see what comes of it." For such a policy as this, once introduced, could hardly be reversed without giving rise to much bitterness of feeling. We have to do, therefore, with a proposal which, if accepted once, is accepted permanently.

---

[1] Mr. Chamberlain's speech at Welbeck.
[2] *Economic Journal*, 1904, p. 27.

" Make a mistake in legislation—it can be corrected. Make a mistake in your Imperial policy — it is irretrievable." [1]

For these reasons the view that a preferential policy would promote Imperial unity, whether political or moral, is not, in my opinion, warranted. Even, however, if this conclusion were reversed, the practical certainty of evil accompaniments to Preference within the United Kingdom itself would still throw a heavy burden of proof upon the advocates of that policy. No doubt our information on the whole subject is painfully imperfect. But when, through the half-lights of inadequate knowledge, warnings of grave disaster gleam, it behoves a statesman to decline adventure, and to dwell in the beaten paths.

[1] Mr. Chamberlain at Birmingham, May 15, 1903, *Speeches*, p. 17.

THE END